T0307884

# Imagism:

# Essays on Its Initiation, Impact and Influence

Edited by
John Gery, Daniel Kempton,
and H. R. Stoneback

Ezra Pound Center for Literature Book Series: No. 5

**UNO PRESS**

Printed in the United States of America

Edited by John Gery, Daniel Kempton, and H. R. Stoneback
*Imagism: Essays on Its Initiation, Impact and Influence*

ISBN: 978-1-60801-113-1
Library of Congress Control Number: 2013940048
Copyright © 2013 by UNO Press

Cover Art:
*The Café Royal*, 1911, Charles Ginner (1878-1952), Oil on canvas
©Tate, London 2013

# UNO PRESS

All rights reserved.
University of New Orleans Press
unopress.org

# The Ezra Pound Center for Literature

The Ezra Pound Center for Literature Book Series is a project dedicated to publishing a variety of scholarly and literary works relevant to Ezra Pound and Modernism, including new critical monographs on Pound and/or other Modernists, scholarly studies related to Pound and his legacy, edited collections of essays, volumes of original poetry, reissued books of importance to Pound scholarship, translations, and other works.

**Series Editor:** John Gery, University of New Orleans

## Editorial Advisory Board

## Ezra Pound Center for Literature Book Series

# Contents

## III. Influence

## Afterword

## Notes on Contributors

## Index

# Foreword

This collection has resulted from the genuine collaboration of its three editors and thirteen contributors in the course of a half decade. In December 2006, off-site from that year's Modern Language Association Convention, at the nearby Franklin Club in Philadelphia, two fervent Poundians, Emily Mitchell Wallace and Gregory Harvey, arranged a remarkable banquet in celebration of six modernist poets with close ties to Pennsylvania—Wallace Stevens, William Carlos Williams, Ezra Pound, H.D., Robinson Jeffers, and Marianne Moore. In the midst of the numerous courses, many tributes to the poets, and even more poems, poet and critic H. R. Stoneback, as requested by Wallace, delivered his formal toast to Pound. But between dessert and a further round of toasts, poet and critic John Gery, Founding Director of the Ezra Pound Center for Literature at the University of New Orleans and Brunnenburg, Italy, grabbed the chance to meet Stoneback for the first time in person. The two had previously developed a correspondence, and earlier that year Stoneback had proposed to Gery the idea of holding a conference devoted to Imagism at Brunnenburg, the castle in northern Italy where Pound's daughter, Mary de Rachewiltz, and her son, Walter de Rachewiltz, have lived most of their lives. Hoping the occasion might give rise for an "Imagist Reunion" between Mary de Rachewiltz and Catherine Aldington, Richard Aldington's daughter, Stoneback offered that the meeting be held in conjunction with the biennial conference of the International Richard Aldington Society, which he and Daniel Kempton have co-directed since 2000. Gery eagerly concurred.

In short, despite that poor health kept Catherine Aldington, sadly, from making the trip from France to Italy that summer, the first meeting of a lively new conference devoted to the history, criticism, and practice of Imagism convened in early July, stirring new found interest in this little studied yet pivotal modernist movement. It included a plenary address by William Pratt, prominent Imagist scholar and editor of *The Imagist Poem: Modern Poetry in Miniature*, as well as papers (or "conversations," as Stoneback preferred to call them) by Mary de Rachewiltz, Marie-Brunette Spire, daughter of the French poet Andre Spire ("Spire thanked me in proposito," writes Pound in Canto 116), and such accomplished scholars as, among others, Emily Mitchell Wallace, Michael Copp, Ian MacNiven, and Kempton (a medievalist who also works in modernist studies). For the occasion, eminent Poundian Tim Redman prepared a bibliography of Imagist holdings at Brunnenburg. Later, many of the best papers, edited by Stoneback, appeared in *Florida English*, Volume 6 (2008), thanks to the efforts of its editors, Courtney Ruffner and Jeff Grieneisen.

Indeed, the enthusiasm for and success of the first Imagism conference led Stoneback, with Kempton's assistance, to organize a second, larger conference three years later in July 2010, again at Brunnenburg. Stoneback worked in close collaboration with Gery, who that year was celebrating the twentieth anniversary of the Pound Center's summer seminars at Brunnenburg with a small group of distinguished alumni. Again, though with an even wider sweep of participants, the meeting featured an array of distinguished papers on Imagism, on the various Imagists, and on modernism, together with poetry readings, a tea with Mary, an evening of one of Walter de Rachewiltz's legendary wine tastings, a conference banquet, a tour of nearby Schloss Tirol (one of the oldest extant castles in Europe), and yet more "conversations" over memorable meals in the nearby village of Dorf Tirol, on benches beside Brunnenburg's orchards and vineyards, or along the steep rise up the mountain from the castle.

During the three-day meeting, Kempton proposed a plan to gather and edit as much of the criticism and scholarship being presented as might be available. The result is this book. A companion volume, *Aldington, Pound, and Imagists at Brunnenburg*, edited by Kempton and Stoneback (Gregau Press, 2012) has also appeared, including in it original poetry read at the conference, as well as criticism on Imagism, Pound, Aldington, H.D. and others, together with newly published Aldington manuscripts.

But the present volume—with its specific focus on the cultural milieu that gave rise to Imagism, the subtle yet sustained impact of Imagism on modernist writing, and Imagism's influence extending to works of two writers not usually linked to the movement—means both to acknowledge the first century of Imagism's continuing presence across the spectrum of literature in English (as well as an array of other languages) and to lay some groundwork for further critical research on this movement that will not fade, it seems, anytime soon.

*     *     *

In its division into three sections, this collection means to suggest by example the inherent value of approaching Imagism and its poetry historically, analytically, and aesthetically. These essays are framed by an Introduction by Helen Carr and an Afterword by Stoneback, based on his keynote address at the 2010 conference. Carr's recent book, *The Verse Revolutionaries: Ezra Pound, H.D. and the Imagists*, has become, and will be for the foreseeable future, the definitive critical history of the Imagist poets. In her essay here, she reconsiders the heritage of critical thinking about Imagism from its inception up to the recent past, especially surrounding the sometimes contradictory speculation on the movement's political dimensions.

Then Part I offers four essays examining the cultural and intellectual context of the beginnings of *Imagisme*: first, Christos Hadjiyiannis examines Pound's Imagist "theory," such as it was, in relation to contemporaneous thinking on the subject by T. E. Hulme and Edward Storer (as well as F. S. Flint) in the years leading up to the first Imagist anthology, *Des Imagistes*, as Hadjiyiannis positions Imagism as abetting both the ideological refutation of romanticism among critics at the time of its inception and, obversely, the "beginning of modern 'classicism.'" Then Justin Kishbaugh critiques Pound's editorial strategies in devising the *Des Imagistes* anthology itself, as Kishbaugh argues for Pound's applying a more wide-ranging aesthetic than the classical Greek and early Asian background usually associated with Imagist technique, in order that the anthology "reveal… the defining aspects of his Imagist program" not as derivative only from ancient Greek and early Asian sources, but as a "confluence" of a wide array of sources and contexts from which original poetry can best spring. Focusing mainly on Pound, Anderson Araujo next traces the telling aspects of Imagism— notably, for instance, as "a rather austere, lean poetic aesthetic"—that remained central to the dynamic principles of Pound's and Wyndham Lewis's Vorticist movement (which erupted in London even as Imagism was just becoming acknowledged). Then, at the close of Part I, Shelley Puhak turns a little further outward culturally, as she reflects on Pound's keen awareness of scientific developments early in the century; in particular, she examines the new uses of the photographic lens, upon which Pound seizes not only as metaphoric premise for Imagist poetry, but as a paradigm for the poet himself as a "radiant node" of light perfectly aligned to the camera lens in service of a scientific observation of the world.

Part II includes four more essays, but here the authors delve into Imagism as a cultural and artistic force: Alex Shakespeare considers the music and musicality of Imagist poetry, as Pound thought about it, both in terms of *vers libre* (the "musical sequence" of Imagist technique) and of the relationship of avant-garde music to poetry itself, innovative in its "ideas about tone, rhythm, and harmony," especially in the years leading to World War I. In contrasting Imagism with another powerful movement, Impressionism, Max Saunders investigates Pound's writing relationship with "an improbable Imagist," namely, Ford Madox Ford, who had greatly influenced Pound's early poetry but also championed Imagism, in spite of his Impressionist style in his own poetry, which Saunders defines. John Gery next argues for the inherently contradictory signification of two of the early Imagist principles, the precision of image (*phanopoeia*) and the concision of meaning (*logopoeia*); but he goes on to demonstrate how in successful Imagist poems—most notably, those by H.D.—this evidently irreconcilable conflict in Pound's Imagist theory dissolves in the execution of the poetry itself as "provocatively ambiguous." Then J. T. Welsch, in his essay on William Carlos Williams's resistance to Imagist principles, also focuses on its theoretical shortcomings, particularly in how Williams was to find more inspiration from the visual artists of the 1913 Armory Show and Alfred Kreymborg's *Others* than from the literary movement on the other side of the Atlantic from where Williams lived. Yet by tracing the evolving nature of Williams's critique of Imagism, Welsch contends that the poet arrived at his critical position only after twenty years or more of shaping his own poetics, suggesting that the early Williams was indeed more closely tied to Imagism than he would later concede.

In Part III, thinking of Imagism's legacy, three writers take up separate cases for Imagism's influence outside the London circle. In his essay, Brad McDuffie first acknowledges Pound's impact on Ernest Hemingway's prose in general but then argues specifically for the Imagist precedent as the operating aesthetic behind the innovative style of Hemingway's first, groundbreaking collection of stories, *In Our Time*. Such distinctive devices in this book as structural "convergence," the layering or "super-positioning" of imagery, and the "symbolic" resonance of images and even words, McDuffie observes, derive directly from Imagism's innovative premises. Roy Verspoor, in identifying other, though related qualities from the early Imagist perspective, finds considerable merit in the case for Imagism as a shaping force on Hemingway's determination in the 1920s to develop an incisive style with an "objective" treatment of his subject matter, even in fiction. Yet Verspoor goes further to assert that, in *The Torrents of Spring*, Hemingway's satiric novella written shortly after *In Our Time*, his excessive, overly sentimental writing is deliberately parodic and, in fact, can be read as a *negative* model of the excessive style Pound warns against in his list of dicta in his 1913 statement, "A Few Don'ts" (reprinted in "A Retrospect" in 1918). Finally, Ian MacNiven presents strong evidence of the movement's expanding influence, when he illustrates how, at the further remove of a full generation after Imagism flowered, James Laughlin's own poetry changed dramatically as a result of his interaction with the Imagist techniques he learned from Pound. While the often self-deprecating Laughlin did lay claim to introducing his own "typewriter metric" into his poetry, nonetheless, the mark of his best verse, as MacNiven illustrates, remains rooted in Imagist thinking, earning him the appellation, "unacknowledged Imagist."

In his Afterword, Stoneback seals the case virtually all this volume's authors imply about the dynamic reach of Imagism, but he does so through memoir: Through his early exposure to church hymns and his involvement with a young woman from Crawfordsville, Indiana, who could relate to him the town's lore about its one-time (though short-lived) most notorious resident, Ezra Pound, Stoneback recalls this early experience as his own initiation into both Pound and Imagism. But then he "leaps" from Indiana to China in the 1980s, where by chance he was to encounter one of the most far-flung of Pound's protégés—former Pound student at Wabash and scholar, Robert Winter, who had left Crawfordsville on Pound's advice shortly after 1908 to go and live in China and, from all accounts, had never returned. Not only does Stoneback pay artistic tribute to Winter (whose own writings and papers may have been lost after his death not long after Stoneback met him) for what the younger writer learned from him, including Winters's thoughts on Imagism, but the picture Stoneback provides us of the iconoclastic Winter, discovered suddenly as "a man floating on his back puffing away at a cigarette" in the middle of Kunming Lake, by the Summer Palace in Beijing, becomes an Imagist poem in its own right. In a manner not difficult to discern, Winter's Imagistic "conversations" with Stoneback from 1984 are now in extended discourse with the critics and scholars found throughout this book, just as their work on Imagism means to extend that discourse into conversations yet to occur.

\*     \*     \*

In compiling and completing this book, the editors would like to thank Mary de Rachewiltz, Walter de Rachewiltz, and Brigitte de Rachewiltz, as well as the next generation of Pound heirs, Michael and Nicholas de Rachewiltz, for their readiness to open their home at Brunnenburg not once but twice in three years, allowing the contributors to and editors of this collection to meet and nurture each others' ideas. Gratitude is also due to this volume's contributors for their prompt attention to editorial details, their receptive and cooperative exchanges through the long process of publication, and their great patience, as well as to each of the members of the Ezra Pound Center for Literature Book Series Editorial Advisory Board for their sustaining advice, good sense, and encouragement, especially Marjorie Perloff, David Moody, Ira Nadel, and Demetres Tryphonopoulas. Thanks also to Bill Lavender, former editor and publisher at UNO Press, for his unflagging support and encouragement of this project and other titles in the EPCL Book Series during the years he nurtured the press from its infancy. At the University of New Orleans, those who have made substantial contributions to the Pound Center and to assuring that this collection would make it into print include Alea Morelock-Cot, Assistant Vice President of International Education; former Dean of Liberal Arts Susan Krantz; Jennifer Stewart, former Pound Center administrator and

Brunnenburg planner for several important years; Peter Schock, Chair of the Department of English; and Pound Center student associates Brendan Frost, Kelly Anne Jones, and Kat Stromquist. Finally, thanks to the hardworking staff at UNO Press, including Editor Abram Himelstein, and graduate assistants Kara Breithaupt, Lauren Capone, and Allison Reu, for their ever ready energy and optimism during a difficult period of transition for the press.

The Editors

# Introduction

# Imagism: A Hundred Years On

Helen Carr

When Ezra Pound first named and vigorously promoted *les Imagistes* in the years before World War I, he presented them simultaneously as the latest poetic movement and as the custodians of the best poetic practice of the past. Imagism was to be both avant-garde in its rejection of the status quo and anti-avant-garde in its desire to preserve the greatest achievements of other ages and, significantly, of other places. Pound's naming of the Imagists was, as contributors here point out, an event now recognised as the opening salvo, the *point de repère* in T. S. Eliot's famous phrase, of Anglo-American modernism. So perhaps it is not surprising that Pound's program for Imagism included in embryo some of the contradictions and complexities of the later movement. But while Pound may have named the movement, Imagism was, as his fellow Imagist F. S. Flint later said, "like all other literary movements . . . a general movement, a product and impulse of the time" (Middleton 43). Other poets were involved, often with rather different views of the significance of this new poetic, with its dense simplicity, pared concentration, and sharp evocations. One of the pleasures of this collection of essays on Imagism is that the different contributors open up a striking variety of readings of the different strands, poetic aims, and influences of this multi-faceted poetic moment. If Pound defined the image as "that which presents an intellectual and emotional complex in an instant of time," something of the same could be said of the birth of the

Imagist movement ("A Few Don'ts" 200).

This is, I believe, the first time a book of essays has been published on
the Imagists, though there have been several monographs. Its appearance
is well timed, a century on from when the movement was first launched,
an apt moment to look again at the turbulent poetic scene in London in the
years before the Great War and to assess its legacy. During the decades in
literary criticism when high modernism held canonical sway, Imagism was
frequently dismissed as an unimportant phase, a "red herring" as Hugh
Kenner put it, of some significance perhaps in Pound's story, but not often
beyond (58).[1] Modernist studies are very different today, recuperating
neglected figures and moments, aware of the plurality of modernisms,
and recognizing much more that modernist writing both registered and
participated in the seismic political and cultural changes of the first half
of the twentieth century. In this rather different intellectual climate, the
remarkable cultural explosion that was Imagism can perhaps be understood
in different and more diverse ways. Imagist poetry has always been popular
with readers, possibly one reason why New Critics looked askance at it,
but critically it remains controversial, a tribute, perhaps, to its continued
power.

The political implications of Imagism have in particular been an
arena of controversy. Given that Pound was Imagism's definer and
impresario, can his later politics, some have asked, be found in embryo
in the movement itself? When I wrote my own book on the Imagists, *The
Verse Revolutionaries*, I wanted to argue that, on the contrary, what was
significant about the movement in political terms was its shared structure
of feeling (to use Raymond Williams's phrase) with the revolutionary social
and political demands for change that were being made at the same time,
sometimes noisily, always insistently, by socialists, suffragettes, anarchists,
anti-colonialists and many others. They showed a similar impatience with
the established order, and anger against a moribund system of authority
sanctioned by custom but not merit, a system that in much of Europe was
soon to collapse. I wanted to stress "the sudden sense of liberation" that
this poetic brought with it as it eschewed the conventional, the wordy, the
ornate, or the bland, for a spare intensity. Yet others have seen Imagism
more as the seedbed of later totalitarianism. These two views are not
necessarily incompatible—revolution can turn rapidly into reaction—and,
it is certainly true, as Christos Hadjiyiannis here points out, that some of

those associated with Imagism besides Pound were already developing ideas that in retrospect could be seen as proto-fascist. Of course, to suggest that early modernism was liberatory and later modernism authoritarian is nothing new. That story has been told in detail in Michael Levenson's *The Genealogy of Modernism*. But that isn't the only story; not all modernisms turned reactionary, and not all Imagists became fascists. H.D.—and Pound, one should remember, said more than once that he invented the movement to launch her poetry—certainly did not, nor did Richard Aldington, nor the life-long socialist Flint. Amy Lowell, definitely a rebel against the conventions of Boston womanhood if not against its distribution of wealth, did not live long enough for definitive claims to be made, but it seems highly unlikely she would have dropped her warm support for either American capitalism or its version of democracy. In the years when the cataclysm of the war and its aftermath scarred the psyche and transformed the map of Europe, it is true that many political positions hardened. Some of those more obviously political pre-war anarchists and revolutionaries became supporters of totalitarianism, left or right, yet like the Imagists, by no means all moved that way.

One early proponent of this grimly teleological reading of Imagism was the young Donald Davie, who in 1952 insisted that "the development from Imagism in poetry to fascism in politics is clear and unbroken" (99).[2] When Davie wrote this, there was only one story of modernism, centring on the men of 1914, and it is to his credit that at a time when most critics strove to evade or ignore their reactionary politics, he faced them so squarely. Yet what Davie argued was so politically dangerous about Imagist poetry was, perhaps surprisingly, its abandonment of syntax; "it is impossible," he writes,

> not to trace a continuity between the laws of syntax and the laws of society, between bodies of usage in speech and in social life, between tearing a word from its context and choosing a leader out of the ruck. One could almost say, on this showing, that to dislocate syntax in poetry is to threaten the rule of law in the civilized community. (99)

An extreme reaction, one might feel, to unorthodox language use: what would Davie imagine to be the political consequences of text messaging?

Yet Pound himself increasingly argued there was a connection between the right use of language and the good society, though for him the Imagist insistence on the exact word was what guaranteed its power. But Davie is here, it seems, equating syntax and reasoned thought, and pointing to the association of fascism and irrationality, with its demagogue leaders and appeal to mythic concepts of blood and soil. He is not the only critic to conclude that Pound's pre-poststructuralist view of language, his embrace of the ideogrammic method, and his fascism are all of a piece.[3] Yet in practice, Imagist poetry rarely eschews syntax as such, and surely no poetic form, syntactical or otherwise, simply appeals to abstract reason. If Walter Benjamin recognised the danger of fascism's aestheticization of politics, poetry is in the broadest sense inevitably aesthetic: it never works purely by ratiocination, which is what gives it its power, for good or evil. As John Gery argues so cogently here, Imagism draws together "sense and sensation," "logopoeia" and "phanopoeia," or, as in Pound's crucial Imagist formulation, "intellect and emotion."

What Davie appears to mean by dislocation of syntax, and to find so perilous, is the Imagist use of parataxis, certainly foundational in Pound's construction of *The Cantos*, and something that enters Imagism most characteristically through the haiku form, in which two apparently heterogeneous images are laid side by side, without any overt cupola or syntactical link. Davie is reading backwards from Pound's later and more disturbing certainties, and from the discontinuities of *The Cantos*, to suggest that these brief and delicate epiphanies presage Pound's fascist convictions. The most famous Imagist poem, "In a Station of the Metro," described by Pound as "hokku-like," is, as it happens, one of the few without a main verb, so perhaps open, Davie would think, to the charge of syntactical, and hence societal, sabotage:

The apparition of these faces in the crowd;
Petals on a wet, black bough. (*Personae* 111)[4]

These two lines, bringing together the urban west and the painterly east, the ancient underworld and the modern metropolis, form perhaps a companion piece to "The Return," one of Pound's first identifiably Imagist poems. Pound's vision in that poem of the return of the ancient gods of poetry to the modern world is enacted here; he has found a poetic form that can convey this epiphanic, momentary glimpse of evanescent beauty in the city crowd. But fascist? It is undoubtedly true that one can find extra-poetic statements by Pound at this time where his faith in the absolute rightness of his intuitive judgments, or his use of aggressively masculinist language, can be read as early intimations of how his politics would move. But I think Davie is wrong to attach that to Imagist poetry as a whole.

Yet Davie is not the only critic to see the haiku as a dangerous model. Daniel Tiffany, whose book *Radio Corpse* also links Imagism and fascism, writes that "the influence of Japanese haiku on Imagism . . . can be understood as an exotic means of formalizing and dignifying a poetic suicide . . . the haiku form permits European (or Anglo-American) poetry to take its own life publicly, in a manner that implicates other dimensions of Western culture but is not fully intelligible (since it is foreign)" (49). Tiffany, it appears, sees the embrace of the haiku's brevity as a suicidal gesture of despair, a capitulation that etiolates and attenuates the Imagists' verse so that it becomes merely spectral, the ghost of poetry, mirroring the self-immolation and self-inflicted death of fascist Europe. Yet Imagism, and its embrace of the haiku, far from killing Anglo-American poetry, led to a fresh burst, indeed a new birth of poetic production, not just in Britain and America, but beyond. Davie and Tiffany are surely right, of course, that poetic form has political implications and that there can be a connection between the laws of society and those of prosody. Yet the laws, or one might say conventions, of society can become corrupt, and changing prosody can be one way of challenging them: it is possible to read the politics of Imagist verse in other terms.

Imagism was conceived on the eve of four dark decades of western history, and for both Davie and Tiffany its poetry is implicated in the darkness that followed its conception. Imagist poetry registers the disruptions of its moment, the intimations of a radically inchoate world, but it is surely rather a critique of what led to those terrible years than a prefiguration. Imagism in its reach of influences and sources (many of which were indeed, as Tiffany suspiciously notes, "foreign") implicitly rejected nineteenth-century nationalism, imperialism, and the belief in the superiority of western modernity, ideas that played a powerful role in the genesis of the First World War and that were later central to fascism. Imagism, as I've argued elsewhere, draws on the ancient past and on non-western forms, something Anderson D. Araujo underlines in his essay here.[5] I was delighted to be introduced by this essay to Wallace Stevens's comment, "Imagism is an ancient phase of poetry. It is something permanent." That was certainly what Pound and H.D. aimed to make their readers feel, something they had in common with artists like Jacob Epstein, of whose sun-god Pound wrote home enthusiastically that it "might have been exkavited from Babylon & not questioned as to authenticity' (Pound, *Letters* 277). Yet much Imagist poetry also registers a rapidly changing and technologically driven metropolis: in his short book on Imagism, Andrew Thacker charts a range of Imagist poems (including Pound's Metro 'hokku') about tube trains and city transport, and several scholars, including Shelley Puhak here, have pointed to their fascination with scientific change.[6] The haiku, I have and would continue to claim, gave to Imagism the poetic equivalent of the collage form, whose unexpected juxtapositions, James Clifford argues in his essay on the surrealists, grew out of a new consciousness of the fragmented heterogeneity of a world of multiple and conflicting cultures.[7] Michel Foucault (not someone often quoted in the context of the Imagists) said of the twentieth century, "We are in the epoch of simultaneity: we are in the epoch of juxtaposition, the epoch of the near and the far, of the side-by-side, of the dispersed." The Imagists in their paratactic, pared-down verse, evoke that simultaneity, what Pound called "super-position," near and far, old and new brought together; they fuse inner subjectivity and the outside world, registering "the precise instant when a thing outward and objective transforms itself, or darts into a thing inward and subjective ("Vorticism" 281).

Pound and his fellow Imagists were concerned with what he called "world-poetry," past and present. Translation, or perhaps one should say the reworking of other poems from other languages, was central to their poetry.[8] Their knowledge of "world-poetry" was necessarily limited, generally second-hand and often erroneous, but they were imaginatively internationalists; they saw past and present as a web of connections, not a forward march. Imagism was an urban phenomenon, and Raymond Williams has argued that modernism emerges from the "miscellaneity" of the modern metropolis; people from widely different class and cultural backgrounds coming together, meeting new ideas and possibilities, imperial centres drawing people from all over the world (45). Crucially there emerged in the modern metropolis a new consciousness of the wider, global world, heterogeneous and hybridised, and it is a consciousness the

Imagists embrace. To return to Pound's apparently anti-avant-garde claim that the Imagists only continue the best of the past, it was a refigured, transcultural and, one might say, avant-garde version of the past.

Yet Imagism has also been attacked not only for its politics but for its lack of them. James Longenbach, like Daniel Tiffany, sees in Imagist brevity a kind of defeat, what he calls a "diminished aesthetic," a disconsolate romanticism, which Pound eventually threw over because it was also "implicitly feminized" (107, 119). "Diminished" is not an adjective that Pound would have recognized, of course. His definition of the image is one of concentration, maximum aesthetic power: "less is more" is one of the crucial insights of many branches of modernist art. As the first Flint/Pound account of *Imagisme* claimed, "Art is all science, all religion, philosophy and metaphysic" (Middleton 38). Nothing diminished there, though it is true they don't explicitly mention politics, which for Longenbach is their weakness. Longenbach certainly sees no intimations of fascism in this "feminized" form, on the contrary suggesting it was a limitation of Imagism that it prevented Pound from "speak[ing] meaningfully of contemporary culture" (108). Longenbach's argument is, briefly put, that early twentieth-century poets, including the Imagists, wanted "to limit poetry's terrain," but when the war confronted them with "an epic subject," poets were compelled, even if "suspicious of their own achievement," to respond in epic terms (103, 109). Writing that rejected epic forms and engagement with large public events he calls "feminized," describing it in Virginia Woolf's words as writing that "ranged among almost unknown or unrecorded things; it lighted on small things and showed perhaps they were not small after all" (115). Woolf's words are certainly an apt description of Imagism, and indeed of the way much successful poetry works. But for Longenbach, to be "feminized" is apparently a defect, given that he describes the Imagists as "poets who needed to condense the universe of poetry into a space so small that it threatened to seem almost precious" (106). He allows that Imagism works for H.D., for whom "that preciousness became a kind of weapon... Erected during the First World War, when militarism and masculinity seemed to go hand in hand, H.D's lyric world was a strategic rejection of an epic imperative" (106).

Is Imagism a 'feminized' poetic form? This is an intriguing suggestion, but I think the gendering of Imagist poetry could be said to work in more complex ways. For women like H.D. and Lowell, one of the advantages of the direct speaking voice of an Imagist poem was that the gender of the speaker could be left ambiguous. What is the gender of the speaker of "Hermes of the Ways"? What is the gender of the speakers of Lowell's powerful love poems, like, for example, "In the Garden" or "The Taxi"? H.D.'s Imagist poetry can take a traditional "feminine" emblem like the rose, and transform it:

> Rose, harsh rose,
> marred and with stint of petals,
> meagre flower, thin,
> sparse of leaf . . .
> Can the spice-rose
> drip such acrid fragrance
> hardened in a leaf? (5)

No comment, no argument, just, as Pound would say, presentation, but it recreates the terms in which the feminine can be understood. Longenbach is right that H.D. is anti-war, opposed to militarized masculinity, but that does not mean she is retreating to a "feminized" form, if by "feminized" is meant a retreat from the political; opposition to militarism is a political stance. Both H.D. and Amy Lowell want to escape from the conventional femininity of their day, and the concentrations and directness of Imagism enable them to do so. The enormous popularity among young American women in the years following its publication of Lowell's poem "Patterns" (1917), an anti-war poem that is also a protest against the gendered constrictions of convention, suggests that readers recognised that; it was the favorite poem of the anthropologists Margaret Mead and Ruth Benedict, and a potent influence on their thinking.

But how would one see the gendering of the male Imagists' poems, particularly Pound's? Pound's extra-poetic comments can appear to stress a virile toughness ("hard, clear edges," "more like granite," and so on), but the poems themselves don't necessarily work like that. I wouldn't want to call them "feminized" as Longenbach does. It's more that, as with Lowell and H.D., the Imagist form can allow a voice that isn't limited to a conventional masculine timbre; perhaps it is more what Virginia Woolf called "androgynous," granite *and* rainbow. Pound sometimes explicitly uses a female voice, as in his version of Lady Ban's poem:

O fan of white silk,
            clear as frost on the grass-blade.
You also are laid aside. (*Personae* 111)

Precise, delicate, and poignant—those are qualities that are present in many of his poems at this time drawn from Far Eastern sources. His *Cathay* poems are war poems in the sense that they are poems about the pity of war, not any masculinist celebration of it. But they are undoubtedly, I would argue, contra Longenbach, political poems.

There is, I think, a similar dichotomy between T. E. Hulme's belligerent critical rhetoric and his evocation of human vulnerability in the poems that Flint described as his "little Japanese pictures." I have placed particular emphasis here on the Imagist debt to the far east; I am not discounting the importance of their other sources—Greek, French, Irish and others— explored here by Justin Kishbaugh in his analysis of *Des Imagistes*. As Kishbaugh suggests, Imagism comes out of their fusion. Yet after these critiques of Imagist brevity, and of the way the Imagists, like the Japanese poets, "lighted on small things," even if they "showed perhaps they were not small after all," I want to end with the Irish poet Seamus Heaney's very different assessment of what the Imagists gained from the haiku. Heaney suggests that although Pound did not follow its formal rules, in his "*hokku*-like" poems the haiku's "sense of evanescence, of the transitoriness of things, of the stillness behind things into which they eventually pass, this essential quality is nevertheless present" (215). Writing of "In a Station of the Metro," "the briefest but most influential poem in [Pound's] total oeuvre," Heaney says:

Thanks to these fourteen words, we are now well attuned to the Japanese effect, the evocation of that precise instant of perception, and are ready to grant such evocation of the instant a self-sufficiency of its own. We don't require any labouring of the point. We are happy if the image sets off its own echoes and associations, if it speaks indirectly, as Issa speaks in his haiku: "A good world - / dew drops fall / by ones by twos." (214-15)

The Imagists, he suggests, drew from the Japanese the concept of *mono no aware*, the "pathos of things," which "refers to sadness or melancholy arising from a deep empathic appreciation of the ephemeral beauty manifested in nature, human life or a work of art" (215). What later poets have learnt through the Imagists or more directly from Japanese poetry is a new honesty and humanity:

> in the course of the twentieth century, as empires and ideologies contended for supremacy, and atrocities were committed on a scale unprecedented in human history, poets became desperately aware of the dangers of rhetoric and abstraction. In these circumstances, the poet's duty to be truthful became more and more imperative, and as it did, the chastity and reticence of Japanese poetry grew more and more attractive. Its closeness to common experience and its acknowledgement of mystery, its sensitivity to *lacrimae rerum*, to the grievous aspects of human experience, have made it a permanent and ever more valuable resource to which other literatures can turn. (218)

Pound did later feel compelled, as James Longenbach says, to turn to the epic form, though John Gery is surely right when he says the Imagist aesthetic remained with Pound throughout *The Cantos*, as it does in H.D.'s major poems such as *Trilogy*. So too did their awareness of *mono no aware*, the "pathos of things."

Imagism can be seen, as T. S. Eliot said, as the point of departure for the development of Anglo-American modernist verse, and also, as some contributors argue here, for modernist prose. Yet the Imagists themselves looked backwards, and outwards, to other times and other cultures, to understand poetry's place and their own in the modern world. As F. S. Flint said of the Tour Eiffel school of images, they shared a dissatisfaction with the present—he stresses the state of poetry but it was also with the state of world. Poetically, the Imagists valued spare intensity, but the movement itself was a complex, multifaceted, many-stranded one; the image was, in one sense, an attempt to make the complexities of modern life cohere. The essays in this welcome collection explore many of these issues, the evolution of Imagism, its politics, its poetics and its legacy, and offer new and intriguing insights into this simultaneously revolutionary and, in the best sense, *passéiste* movement.

## Notes

1. Some are still dismissive of Imagism: Lawrence Rainey, for example, with his attention to the cultural economy of modernism, sees Imagism as purely anti-avant-garde and more a marketing strategy than anything else (30).

2. From *The Purity of Diction in English Verse*, London: Routledge & Kegan Paul, 1952, p. 99. Interestingly, it is not a charge that he repeats in his excellent 1974 *Pound*, in the Fontana Modern Masters series.

3. See, for example, Alan Durrant, *Ezra Pound: Identity in Crisis*, and Maud Ellmann, *The Poetics of Impersonality*.

4. Some very brief poems by Hulme and Storer also lack main verbs. Rupert Richard Arrowsmith suggests that the second line "In a Station of the Metro" takes its image from a Hokusai illustration of "the contrast between the pale, fallen *hanami* petals and rain-wet cherry wood" (122). See also the illuminating discussion of this poem in Alex Shakespeare's essay here.

5. See my essay "Imagism and Empire."

6. See Thacker's chapter on "Modern Themes" in his recent book, *The Imagist Poets*.

7. See Clifford's "On Ethnographic Surrealism" in *The Predicament of Culture*, and Carr, "Imagism and Empire."

8. Much of Imagist poetry is what the influential French art critic Nicolas Bourriaud has called "postproduction" art, the reworking of what already exists.

## Works Cited

Arrowsmith, Richard. *Modernism and the Museum: Asian, African, and Pacific Art and the London Avant-Garde*, Oxford: Oxford UP, 2011. Print.

Bourriaud, Nicolas. *Postproduction. Culture as Screenplay: How Art Reprograms the World*. New York: Lucas & Sternberg, 2002. Print.

Carr, Helen. "Imagism and Empire." *Modernism and Empire*. Ed. Howard J. Booth and Nigel Rigby. Manchester: Manchester UP, 2000. 64-92. Print.

Clifford, James. *The Predicament of Culture: Twentieth-Century Ethnography, Literature, and Art*. Cambridge, MA: Harvard UP, 1988. Print.

Davie, Donald. *The Purity of Diction in English Verse*. London: Routledge and Kegan Paul, 1952. Print.

Durrant, Alan. *Ezra Pound: Identity in Crisis. A Fundamental Reassessment of the Poet and His Work*. Brighton: Harvester, 1981. Print.

Ellmann, Maud. *The Poetics of Impersonality: T. S. Eliot and Ezra Pound*. Brighton: Harvester, 1987. Print.

Foucault, Michel. "Of Other Spaces." Trans. Jay Miskowiec. *Michel Foucault, info.* n.d. Web. 14 Jan. 2013.

H.D. *H.D. Collected Poems 1912-1944.* Ed. Louis L. Martz. New York: New Directions, 1983. Print.

Heaney, Seamus. "Afterword." *Our Shared Japan: An Anthology of Contemporary Irish Poetry.* Ed. Irene De Angelis and Joseph Wood. Dublin: Dedalus, 2007. 211-18. Print.

Kenner, Hugh. *The Poetry of Ezra Pound.* London: Faber & Faber, 1951. Print.

Levenson, Michael. *The Genealogy of Modernism.* Oxford: Oxford UP, 1984. Print.

Longenbach, James. "Modern Poetry." *The Cambridge Companion to Modernism.* Ed. Michael Levenson. Cambridge: Cambridge UP, 1999. 99-127. Print.

Middleton, Christopher. "Documents on Imagism from the Papers of F. S. Flint." *The Review: A Magazine of Poetry and Criticism* 15 (1965): 35-51. Print.

Pound, Ezra. "A Few Don'ts by an Imagiste." *Poetry* 1.6 (1913): 200-01. Print.

---. *Ezra Pound to His Parents: Letters 1895-1929.* Ed. Mary de Rachewiltz, A. David Moody, and Joanna Moody. Oxford: Oxford UP, 2010. Print.

---. *Personae: The Shorter Poems of Ezra Pound.* Rev. ed. Ed. Lea Baechler and A. Walton Litz. New York: New Directions, 1990. Print.

---. "Vorticism." *Early Writings: Poems and Prose.* Ed. Ira B. Nadel. New York: Penguin, 2005. 278-91. Print.

Rainey, Lawrence. *Institutions of Modernism: Literary Elites and Public Culture.* New Haven: Yale UP, 1996. Print.

Thacker, Andrew. *The Imagist Poets.* Horndon: Northcote House, 2011. Print.

Tiffany, Daniel. *Radio Corpse: Imagism and the Cryptaesthetic of Ezra Pound.* Cambridge, MA: Harvard UP, 1995. Print.

Williams, Raymond. *The Politics of Modernism: Against the New Conformists.* London, Verso, 1989. Print.

# I. Imagism: Initiation

# Ezra Pound, T. E. Hulme, Edward Storer: Imagism as Anti-Romanticism in the Pre-*Des Imagistes* Era

Christos Hadjiyiannis

## Introduction

Despite its short history, Imagism ranks as one of the most influential moments in twentieth-century literary history, this gathering of poets in London in the early 1900s acting, in Eliot's famous words, as the *"point de repère . . .* of modern poetry" ("American Literature and the American Language" 58). Much has been written on Imagism's lasting contribution to the development of literary modernism, with critics from Taupin, Isaacs, Coffman, and Pratt to most recently Carr, all charting the various ways in which Imagism acted as the basis on which modernism developed. In this essay, I am specifically concerned with the period spanning 1908-1913, prior to the publication of *Des Imagistes*, the group's first anthology, in 1914, when Imagism began to take its shape.[1] My focus is specifically on three young aesthetes who, during these formative years, discussed the future of modern poetry, effectively redefining verse along Imagist principles: Ezra Pound, responsible for coining the term *"Imagisme"*; T. E. Hulme, credited by many as the "intellectual father" of the movement; and Edward Storer, according to F. S. Flint, one of the group's leading figures.[2] The overarching aim is to map connections between the ideas of these three poets with an ultimate view to illuminating Pound's tenure as an *Imagiste*. As I show, the theories regarding poetic composition of Hulme and Storer anticipate some of the fundamental principles included in Pound's *Imagisme*. While making a claim that either Hulme or Storer exerted direct influence on Pound would be presumptuous and therefore inaccurate, the similarities in their writings emphasize the significant contribution that Hulme and Storer made toward the development of Pound's early aesthetic claims. More crucially, this essay demonstrates how an examination of Pound's aesthetics from the perspective of the theories of Hulme and Storer leads to an interesting "political" interpretation of *Imagisme*. As well as a rejection of nineteenth-century poetic rhetoric, *Imagisme* can be read in terms of an ideological rejection of Liberal England, underneath which Hulme and Storer detected a general malaise of romanticism. In what follows, I begin by sketching out in detail the continuities between the theories of Pound, Hulme, and Storer, and then proceed in the second part of the essay to offer an interpretation of *Imagisme* as both marking the advent of a new aesthetic and heralding the beginning of modern "classicism," launched by Hulme and Storer in 1910-11 and developed into a fully fledged social and political viewpoint by T. S. Eliot in the 1920s.[3]

## Imagist Poetics

According to the famous triad postulated by Pound in March 1913, the three fundamental precepts of *Imagisme* are directness, precision, and musicality (252).[4] Imagist verse rejects vague symbolisms, instead recognizing that, as Pound puts it, the only "adequate symbol" is the "natural object." According to Pound, the poet must use symbols in a way that "their symbolic function does not obtrude; so that a sense, and the poetic quality of the passage, is not lost to those who do not understand the symbol as such, to whom, for instance, a hawk is a hawk" (259). Moreover, Imagist poetry needs to aim for precision, by which Pound means accurate description. Poetry, thus, as he argues in "A Serious Artist," ought to avoid "elaboration and complication." By making "apt use" of metaphor, it must aim to achieve "swiftness, almost a violence, and certainly a vividness"; or, put otherwise, poetry must "Go in fear of abstractions" (246, 254). In the same essay, Pound also demands that the poet break away from the "stale and hackneyed" meter of old (253). That is not to say that modern poetry must unconditionally be based on *vers libre*, the modern version of which

Pound berated for often lacking "musical structure," but, rather, according to the notion of *melopoeia*, the melody of a poem must try "truly to bear the trace of emotion which the poem . . . is intended to communicate" (253, 244). Use must be made of "assonance and alliteration, rhyme immediate and delayed, simple and polyphonic" (255). Ultimately, all three qualities of Imagist verse combine to form a visual description resulting in an image: an "intellectual and emotional complex" (253). Rid of conventions and ornamentations, Pound's Imagist poet is thus left free to present a "complex" image that "gives that sense of sudden liberation; that sense of freedom from time limits and space limits; that sense of sudden growth, which we experience in the presence of the greatest works of art" (253).

Various critics have noted how in "A Lecture on Modern Poetry" from 1908 Hulme makes similar demands to the ones advocated by Pound in "the spring or summer of 1912" (Pound 252).[5] In short, Hulme's lecture advocates the introduction of a new verse form in poetry designed to be more adept to the "modern spirit"; for "Each age must have its own special form of expression," Hulme argues, "and any period that deliberately goes out of it is an age of insincerity" (51-52). The idea is that in the "modern" times in which Hulme was writing philosophers had rejected the view that there is an "absolute truth." "We no longer believe in perfection," Hulme asserts in his lecture, "either in verse or in thought, we frankly acknowledge the relative" (52-53). From this he jumps to the conclusion that the "tendency" of modern poetry ought to be "towards the production of a general effect," for "this . . . takes away the predominance of metre and a regular number of syllables" (53). The subject matter and the tone of poetry had similarly to change: poetry in modern times, Hulme maintains, "no longer deals with heroic action," but on the contrary aims at the "expression and communication of momentary phrases in the poet's mind" (53). Furthermore, by avoiding "sentimentality" modern poetry expresses "virile thought" (51), thereby departing from the "lyrical impulse" of romantic poets such as Tennyson, Shelley, or Keats (53). All things considered, Hulme suggests that modern poetry is best described as "free verse," cautioning, however, that this is not the same as French *vers libre*; rather, modern poetry compares to *vers libre* only in the sense that it is "clothes made to order, rather than ready-made clothes" (52).

Hulme's "specifications" for modern poetry anticipate the principles laid out by Pound in 1913 in more ways than one. Hulme opposes regular metre for the same reasons as Pound: because it is "cramping, jangling, meaningless and out of place" and because "Into the delicate pattern of images and colour it introduces the heavy, crude pattern of rhetorical verse" (54). Like Pound, Hulme insists that poetry has a lot to learn from the "great revolution in music when for the melody that is one-dimensional music was substituted harmony which moves in two" (54). In "A Few Don'ts," Pound blasts the poets who do not use *vers libre* phrases with a musical structure. Rallying against "marked metre in *vers libres* [*sic*]," which he found "stale and hackneyed" (253), he suggests ways in which the poet can benefit from behaving "as a musician, a good musician, when dealing with that phase of your art which has exact parallels in music" (256). Furthermore, in "A Lecture" Hulme draws a distinction that Pound also endorses in "A Serious Artist," albeit less forcefully, describing how "modern" poetry differs from regular verse or "prose." The defining difference between "poetry" and "prose" in Hulme's view is that whereas "poetry" uses direct presentation (it "deals in images") and, in so doing, "arrests your mind all the time with a picture" (55), "prose" "uses images that have died and become figures of speech," thereby allowing "the mind to run along with the least possible effort to a conclusion" (55; cf. Pound 243-45). Finally, Hulme's demand that modern poetry be made up of a series of solid images presented in juxtaposition is not unlike Pound's idea that the "Image," which constitutes "the poet's pigment" (*Gaudier-Brzeska* 86), "presents an intellectual and emotional complex in an instant of time" (253).

While identifying various similarities (and differences) between the poetics of Hulme and Pound has been the commonplace, the possible connections between the aesthetic projects of these two figures with that of Storer have remained largely unexamined. The few critics who have looked into Storer's writings on poetry have concentrated on the fact that, as Coffman puts it, his "definition of poetry marks him as inclining toward the Symbolist rather than the Hulme concept" (105-06). Even Harmer, who cautions other critics against overlooking the value of Storer's programmatic "Essay" from 1908, asserts that Storer is "a thinker with little gift of style," concluding that although he expressed similar positions regarding blank verse to those of Pound, Storer's argument is weakened by obvious inaccuracies (27).[6] Certainly, Storer's aesthetic exercise varies significantly from the Imagism of Pound, Aldington, or H.D. As Carr rightly points out, the majority of Storer's poetry "has the feel of late nineteenth-

century decadence," its tone remaining "very different . . . from much of
the modernist experiments to come" (159). Pound thought it "ridiculous"
to even compare Storer's "custard" with the "Hellenic hardness of H.D's
poems" (qtd. in Middleton 41). Even if his poetry is not obviously Imagist,
however, Storer's attack on "old" verse warrants him a more influential role
in the development of Imagism than commonly assumed, for it contains
in it propositions that are very similar to the ones included in Hulme's
"Lecture" and in Pound's manifestos.

In "An Essay," appended to his 1908 collection of poetry, *Mirrors
of Illusion*, Storer advocates a "purer" and more effective poetry.[7] He
campaigns for the freeing of modern verse from "the restrictions of rhythm
or rhyme," from the use of which, he writes, "There is no real pleasure to
be derived [but] only a kind of dumb amazement and vague unrest" (81).
Moreover, in line with Hulme and Pound, Storer demands that poetic form
reject "conventions" and "artificialities." As he puts it, "Form should not...
be...a kind of rigid mould into which the poetry is to be poured" (106), the
rationale being that, as he goes on to explain,

> There is no absolute virtue in iambic pentameters as such...
> however well they may be. There is no immediate virtue in
> rhythm or rhyme even. These things are merely means to an
> end. Judged by themselves they are monstrosities of childish
> virtuosity and needless iteration. Indeed, rhythm and rhyme are
> often destructive of thought, lulling the mind into a drowsy kind
> of stupor. (106-07)

Thus rejecting the "monstrosities" of metre and rhyme, Storer concludes
that "modern" poetry must be made up of "scattered lines," "descriptions or
suggestions of something at accurate identification . . . convincing enough
to some one portion of the brain" (102).

Storer's demand that poetry must simply aim at giving "convincing"
suggestions, instead of pretending to offer absolute truths, ultimately
rests on his conviction that poetry and reality are "two things [that] are
manifestly self-destructive as mixed by man." It is "only God or the Life-
Force that can mingle these in any successful manner," he argues, adding:
"If we could do so satisfactorily, we should be capable of creating a perfect
image of existence, whereas all we can hope to do is to picture imperfectly

one tiny little portion of it" (82, 102). This belief that it is not the job of the poet to offer "perfect" or "absolute" representations of reality because it is not humanly feasible is, as we have seen above, shared by Hulme (cf. 52-53). Indeed, the conviction that humans are "limited" creatures is what underlies—and unifies—Hulme's and Storer's aesthetic and political projects, revealing a relation of close intimacy between Imagism and Hulme's and Storer's anti-romantic politics.

## Imagism as Anti-Romanticism

During the years 1911-1912, Hulme and Storer launched through the pages of the conservative weekly the *Commentator* a joint attack on everything they saw as "romantic," defining "romanticism" as the belief in human perfection. To counter what they perceived as the general romantic malaise, or, as Storer called it, the "orgy of Romanticism," these two poets proposed that "romanticism" be replaced by "classicism," a general term they used to refer to the position that asserts recognition on the part of humans of their inherent limitations ("The Romantic Conception of History" 170). In the sphere of politics, romanticism is associated with "liberalism" or "socialism," two terms used interchangeably. Storer first argues in the *Commentator* that the belief in progress, seen as the main ideological force behind romanticism, is both false and misleading: it was, as he called it, a "delusion." More importantly for Storer, romanticism in politics is dangerous; for "by glorifying the merely vast and fantastic, [it] has prepared a state of mind among people whereby a political Monstrosity like Socialism could find a more or less ready acceptance among a certain class" ("The Romantic Conception of History" 170). For Hulme, likewise, liberalism or socialism is predicated on the potentially catastrophic belief, epitomized in Rousseau's philosophy, that, as he states in "Romanticism and Classicism," "something positive could come out of disorder" (61). "Here is the root of romanticism," he writes in this programmatic lecture, and "if you can so rearrange society by the destruction of oppressive order then these possibilities will have a chance and you will get Progress" (61).

Having identified romanticism with socialism, Hulme and Storer proceeded to associate classicism, postulated as the only viable alternative, with conservatism. As Hulme explains in "On Progress and Democracy," published in the *Commentator* in August 1911, by contrast to socialism, conservatism does not endorse progress and therefore accepts as a fundamental truth that some forms of order and discipline are needed: "The Conservative does not believe in progress. . . . He believes that man is constant, and that the number and types of the possible forms of society are also constant" (222). Storer puts forward similar propositions. Unlike the liberals and socialists, conservatives, Storer maintains, do not believe that "man is god" and do not valorize the "ideal" over the "real." This is what prevents them from making unrealistic or "fantastic" demands on the state. By contrast to the "theoretical Radical," "the genuine Conservative . . . not only makes the best of things as they are, but accepts with joy the limitations of man" ("The Stage Conservative and the Real One" 155); or, as he puts it in an earlier article, the difference between socialists and conservatives is that "The real Conservative knows that government is much more an affair of the head than of the heart" ("From Democratic Liberalism to Positive Conservatism" 69). Whereas socialism is based on a "sentimentality" that appeals to the socialists' "great but sloppy heart," conservatism "has a keener, more precise outlook, which enables it to pierce the rights and wrongs of individual cases, because it acts coldly and justly" (69).

While denouncing romanticism in politics, Hulme and Storer explicitly paralleled classicism with the Imagist aesthetic. Thus having explained in his *Commentator* articles how the recognition of human limitations implies a conservative political ideology, Hulme moves on in "Romanticism and Classicism" to explain in detail how exactly the classicist ideology is compatible with Imagist poetics. The belief that man is not God and that progress is neither inevitable nor necessarily good, as well as the desire to deal with what *is* rather than what may be—the two defining characteristics of classicist ideology—are quickly translated in Hulme's lecture into a call for dry accuracy and precision in poetry, a rejection of rhetoric and abstract idealism, and an emphasis on the definite rather than the infinite. We therefore read that the "classical poet never forgets this finiteness, this limit of man" (62); instead, "He remembers always that he is mixed up with earth," recognizing "the limits inside which you know man to be fastened," and hence the "classical" poet never moves above "a certain pitch of rhetoric. . . . The kind of thing you get in Hugo or Swinburne" (62-63). Likewise, the essence of the new poetry is "always perfectly human and never exaggerated: man is always man and never a god" (66). Because the classical poet is conscious of the frailties of human nature and therefore "never flies away into the circumambient gas" (61), he tries to describe things in the most accurate and precise way possible. He avoids conventional language, using instead "new metaphors [and] fancy" to make language "precise" (71). By a "concentrated effort of the mind," Hulme's poet expresses "the exact curve of what he sees whether it be an object or an idea in the mind" (69). Ultimately, the "great aim" of classical poetry for Hulme is "accurate, precise and definite description" (68), a process in which the main principles behind Imagism are rendered as the fundamental tenets of modern classicism.

On his part, and in order to counteract what he saw as romanticism in literature, Storer calls in the *Commentator* for a literature based on "a spirit of sane and prosaic reality" ("On Revolution and Revolutionaries" 203). Unlike romanticism, described as based on an "atmosphere of passionate ebullitions, over-heated protests and romantic swan-songs," classicism, Storer claims, is the "enthusiasm" "over things as they are rather than [the] worship and homage to the goddess of things as they never can be" (203). Storer reiterates these claims in the "Introduction" to his edition of Cowper's poems in 1912, an essay that has gone virtually unnoticed by critics.[8] Bemoaning the fact that "romantic art always prefers the extraordinary to the ordinary, the less natural to the natural" and regretting the way that romanticism "would rather deal with the infinite than with the finite," the impulse of romantic poets remaining "perpetually in need of artificial stimulants and allurements," he declares, in line with Hulme, that "There are signs that the Romantic Movement in English poetry has temporarily come to an end" (vii-xi; cf. Hulme 59). Modern poetry, Storer thus concludes, must combine Cowper's "poetic accuracy, the sureness of his observation, and the directness with which he conveys the impression to our minds" (xviii).

Crucially, that which Storer finds in Cowper are also the very qualities that Hulme assigns to modern classical poetry, but they are also a variation of the poetic demands that lie at the basis of Pound's Imagism. Although Pound does not explicitly associate Imagism with classicism, it is significant that Storer's attraction to Cowper echoes Pound's own admiration for Daniel and Cavalcanti in "A Retrospect." For Storer, the lesson from Cowper is that "Only the very clearest kind of vision, the most accurate poetic sense, can . . . make poetry without resorting to that distortion which makes and also mars so much romantic art" ("Introduction" xviii). Pound admits that "In the art of Daniel and Cavalcanti, I have seen that precision which I miss in the Victorians, that explicit rendering, be it of external nature or emotion." "Their testimony," he continues in "A Retrospect," "is of the eyewitness, their symptoms are first hand." And just as Storer claims Cowper as an alternative to the "artificial" impulse of the romantic poet, the "exaggerations and grandeurs" of Shelley, the "impertinent assumptions of divinity with which romantic art abounds," and the "tenderness and sentiment" of "romanticism" ("Introduction" x, xii, xv, xx), so does Pound look to Daniel and Cavalcanti in order to find a way out of the nineteenth century, described in "A Retrospect" as a "rather blurry, messy sort of period, rather sentimentalistic, mannerish sort of a period" (261-62).

## Conclusion

While it does certainly not prove that Pound held similar political convictions to those of either Storer or Hulme, nor that the Imagist aesthetic carries with it a specific political program, an examination of Pound's Imagism vis-à-vis Hulme's and Storer's anti-romanticism contributes to our understanding of Imagism in two important respects. On the one hand, it reminds us of a significant—and often neglected—part of Imagism's history, namely the intimate connection that exists between the Imagist aesthetic and the ideological rejection of "romanticism." On the other hand, and perhaps far more crucially, that Hulme's and Storer's "classicism" went on to become such a rich source of inspiration for the modernists of the 1920s and 1930s verifies as much as it intensifies Eliot's claim that Imagism played an instrumental part toward the development of modernism.

## Notes

1. For a useful and concise history of Imagism, see Nicholls 166-74.

2. Critics who have found Hulme to be a guiding force behind Imagism include Hynes xviii, Harmer 30, Jones 35, Coffman 68, Zach 228-42, Ferguson 63, and Wacior 12, 16. Flint described Storer's contribution to the development of Imagism in "The History of Imagism" (70).

3. See, for example, Eliot, "To Criticize the Critic" 17, "Mr. P. E. More's Essays" 136, "The 'Pensées' of Pascal" 416n2, and "Second Thoughts about Humanism" 489-90.

4. Unless otherwise indicated, all quotes from Pound are taken from *Early Writings, Poems*

*and Prose.*

5. For a discussion of the chronology of "A Lecture on Modern Poetry," see Schuchard 209-11. On the similarities and differences between Hulme's and Pound's poetics, see Taupin 245, Martin, *New Age under Orage* 156 and "'The Forgotten School of 1909' and the Origins of Imagism" 7-38, Jones 35, Harmer 30, McCormick 116-18, Wacior 26, Ferguson 46, and Carr 376.

6. See also Martin, *The New Age under Orage*. Martin suggests that Storer's experimentations with free verse and rhythm share something with the poetic theory and practice of Hulme. Yet, like Coffman and Harmer after him, Martin finds Storer's poems "more obviously related to contemporary French poetry than those of other members of the forgotten school" (149, 158).

7. *Mirrors of Illusion* was reviewed by Flint for *The New Age* in November 1908, at around the same time as Hulme delivered "A Lecture on Modern Poetry." See Flint, "Recent Verse."

8. As far as I know, no critic, with the notable exception of Carr, has paid attention to Storer's "Introduction" to his book on Cowper. Carr discusses the Introduction very briefly, suggesting that Storer's "comments . . . in his Cowper book . . . predate the savage criticism that Pound himself, rather later, came to make" (380). She does not, however, pursue this observation further.

## Works Cited

Carr, Helen. *The Verse Revolutionaries: Ezra Pound, H. D and the Imagists.* London: Jonathan Cape, 2009. Print.

Coffman, Stanley. *Imagism: A Chapter for the History of Modern Poetry.* New York: Octagon Books, 1972. Print.

Eliot, T. S. "American Literature and the American Language." *To Criticize the Critic and Other Writings.* New York: Farrar, Straus and Giroux, 1965. 43-60. Print.

---. "Mr. P. E. More's Essays." *Times Literary Supplement* 21 Feb. 1929: 136. Print.

---. "The 'Pensées' of Pascal." *Selected Essays.* London: Faber, 1999. 402-16. Print.

---. "Second Thoughts About Humanism." *Selected Essays.* London: Faber, 1999. 481-91. Print.

---. "To Criticize the Critic." *To Criticize the Critic and Other Writings.* New York: Farrar, Straus and Giroux, 1965. 11-26. Print.

Ferguson, Robert. *The Short Sharp Life of T .E. Hulme.* London: Allen Lane, 2002. Print.

Flint, F. S. "Recent Verse." *The New Age* 26 Nov. 1908: 95. Print.

---. "The History of Imagism." *The Egoist: An Individualist Review* May 1915: 70-71. Print.

Harmer, J. B. *Victory in Limbo: A History of Imagism, 1908-1917*. London: Secker and Warburg, 1975. Print.

Hulme, T. E. *The Collected Writings of T. E. Hulme*. Ed. Karen Csengeri. Oxford: Oxford UP, 1994. Print.

Hynes, Samuel. "Introduction." *T. E. Hulme: Further Speculations*. Ed. Samuel Hynes. Minneapolis: U of Minnesota P, 1955. v-xxi. Print.

Isaacs, Jacob. *The Background of Modern Poetry*. London, 1951. Print.

Jones, Alun R. *The Life and Opinions of T .E. Hulme*. London: Victor Gollancz, 1960. Print.

Martin, Wallace. *The New Age under Orage*. Manchester: Manchester UP, 1967. Print.

---. "'The Forgotten School of 1909' and the Origins of Imagism." *A Catalogue of Imagist Poets*. Ed. J. H. Woolmer. New York: Woolmer, 1966. 7-38. Print.

McCormick, John. *The Middle Distance: A Comparative History of American Imaginative Literature, 1919-1932*. New York: Free Press, 1971. Print.

Middleton, Christopher. "Documents on Imagism from the Papers of F. S. Flint." *The Review* 15 (1965): 35-51. Print.

Nicholls, Peter. *Modernisms: A Literary Guide*. Berkeley: U of California P. 1995. Print.

Pound, Ezra. *Early Writings: Poems and Prose*. Ed. Ira B. Nadel. New York and London: Penguin, 2005. Print.

---. *Gaudier-Brzeska: A Memoir*. New York: New Directions, 1970. Print.

Pratt, William, and Robert Richardson, eds. *Homage to Imagism*. New York: AMS Press, 1992. Print.

Schuchard, Ronald. "'As Regarding Rhythm': Yeats and the Imagists." *Yeats: An Annual of Critical and Textual Studies*. Ed. Richard J. Finneran. Ithaca, NY: Cornell UP, 1984. 209-26. Print.

Storer, Edward. "An Essay." *Mirrors of Illusion*. London: Sisley's. 75-115. Print.

---. "From Democratic Liberalism to Positive Conservatism." *The Commentator* 14 Jun. 1911: 68-69. Print.

---. "Introduction." *William Cowper: Selections from Cowper's Works*. Ed. Edward Storer. London: Regent Library, 1912. vii-xxiii. Print.

---. "On Revolution and Revolutionaries." *The Commentator* 8 Feb. 1911: 202-03. Print.

---. "The Romantic Conception of History." *The Commentator* 25 Jan. 1911: 170-71. Print.

---. "The Stage Conservative and the Real One." *The Commentator* 18 Jan. 1911: 154-55. Print.

Taupin, René. *The Influence of French Symbolism on Modern American Poetry*. Trans. William Pratt and Anne Rich Pratt. New York: AMS Press, 1985. Print.

Wacior, Slawomir. *Explaining Imagism: The Imagist Movement in Poetry and Art*. Lewiston, NY: Mellen, 2007. Print.

Zach, Natan. "Imagism and Vorticism." *Modernism 1890-1930*. Ed. M. Bradbury and J. McFarlane. London: Penguin, 1975. 228-42. Print.

# Editorial Images: Des Imagistes and Ezra Pound's Imagist Presentation of Imagism

Justin Kishbaugh

In his 2006 article "Ezra Pound's Poetic Anthologies and the Architecture of Reading," John G. Nichols discusses Pound's editorial decisions in *Des Imagistes* as carefully considered tactical maneuvers that provide readers with an understanding of Imagism based on the defining features and arrangement of its product rather than from any sort of explanatory preface or critical apparatus. Nichols states that as "An anthology of Imagist poems . . . *Des Imagistes*, becomes a poetic manifesto," and continues:

> Without prose interpretive guides, *Des Imagistes* offers readers a range of poems that they must read in relation to one another to determine the parameters of the new artistic movement. The arrangement of the anthology's content makes this comparative analysis easier. The poems are arranged not alphabetically or chronologically but by their thematic and stylistic qualities—for example, poems imitating classical or Asian verse traditions are grouped together. (177)

While I agree with Nichols's assessment that *Des Imagistes* works to define Imagism through the deliberate presentation of its product, I argue that Pound's editorial strategies and the concept of Imagism that he attempts to offer in that anthology were both more involved and intricate than simply grouping poems that "imitat[ed] classical or Asian verse traditions."

Admittedly, Greek and Asian flavors dominate the Imagism Pound offers in *Des Imagistes*, but they are not the only ingredients he uses in that dish, nor does he confine their influence to the meal itself. An experienced gastronome will note the care with which Pound creates the ambiance for that meal in his room choice and table setting, as well as how the French and English accents of the meal enhance and complicate the overall gustatory experience. Furthermore, while a cultured palate may distinguish the individual ingredients Pound employs in the Imagism of *Des Imagistes*, it will also recognize that, as a cumulative experience, this meal takes on its own identity and becomes more than the sum of its parts. Or more specifically, along with, and out of, the conflux of allusions and associations to other poetic traditions, Pound presents his readers with an Image of Imagism in *Des Imagistes* that defines itself not only through its origins and influences, but also through the arrangement of the poets Pound selected for his anthology and the individualistic but varied poetic technique their work showcases.

When opening *Des Imagistes* and leafing through its title pages, the reader has his or her perception of Imagism initially shaped through Pound's choice of title and opening epigraph. While that title, *Des Imagistes*, suggests that the anthology contains the full sum and scope of Imagist writers, its French spelling also seems to establish an immediate connection between Imagism and French Symbolism. "Symbolisme," which predated "Imagisme," had popularized the use of free verse, or *vers libre*, and used its fluctuating rhythms in accordance with its attempts to defamiliarize everyday objects. This avant-garde approach to poetics attracted international attention, and by appropriating his own "ism" and spelling it as though it were also French, Pound subtly acknowledges an affinity between the two schools in such a way that he might procure some of the interest in Symbolism for his own nascent poetic movement while also allowing it to maintain its independence and integrity of design. Although this connection between Symbolism and Imagism may seem rather obvious, it does add a first layer to the complex and associative definition of Imagism that Pound creates and offers with his anthology.

Continuing to define Imagism through the materiality of his anthology, Pound also includes a Greek epigraph on the back of the anthology's first title page. The epigraph, taken from the "Lament for Bion," appears in both its original Greek and in English translation. Notably, for the English version, Pound chose Richard Aldington's translation, titled "The Mourning for Bion,"[1] which reads:

> And she also was of Sikilia and was gay in
>     the valleys of Ætna, and knew the Doric
>     singing. (3)

Although the subject matter of this quotation, when read in the context of the entire poem, concerns the speaker's desire "to continue, in a new song, a vital inheritance," and thereby obliquely introduces the aims of Imagist practice, it also initiates the alignment of Imagism with Greek poetics (Bock 160) and, in particular, with the poet Bion prior to offering any actual Imagist poetry.

This attempt to associate Imagism with the Greek poetic tradition, however, was not new. In a well-known letter to Harriet Monroe, in which Pound introduces her to the work of H.D., he states that H.D.'s poetry is "of the Imagistes" because it is "Objective—no slither; direct—no excessive use of adjectives, no metaphors that won't permit examination. It's straight talk, straight as the Greek!" (*Selected Letters* 11). With this sentiment, Pound demonstrates that even from its earliest beginnings he felt that the attributes of Imagism and Greek poetry are based on similar principles. Moreover, by placing this epigraph at the beginning of the book, Pound not only creates a historical precedent that justifies the major principles of Imagist practice, but also establishes the tone for the heavily Greek-influenced poetry of Aldington and H.D. that follows.

Additionally, the matter of Pound's choosing to begin his anthology with a quotation that concerns the Greek poet Bion of Smyrna presents a complex statement on the Imagists' use of free verse. In "A Visiting Card," Pound states that "no one can become an expert [on metre] without knowing Bion" and that "The study of metre will require an odd half-hour or so with [him]" (*Selected Prose* 323, 328); such comments make the Greek poet an interesting choice for Pound to allude to at the beginning of an anthology that seems to champion the use of free verse. One might also recognize that Pound does not directly quote from the work of Bion, but rather takes the epigraph from a work "on Bion" that focuses on the death of that poet. One might conclude, then, from Pound's association of Bion with meter that this quotation could suggest the death of metrical forms in modern poetry, or— and I think more appropriately— one might view this reference as Pound making an argument for the proper method by which a poet should come to use free verse.

In his 1917 essay "Ezra Pound: His Metric and Poetry," T. S. Eliot asserts that "There are not, as a matter of fact, two kinds of verse, the strict and the free; there is only a mastery which comes of being so well trained that form is an instinct and can be adapted to the particular purpose in hand" (172). He also determines that "Pound's *vers libre* is such as is only possible for a poet who has worked tirelessly with rigid forms and different systems of metric" (167-68). Pound also adds legitimacy to this opinion of himself, when, in a discussion "Re Vers Libre," he states that "progress lies rather in an attempt to approximate classical quantitative metres (NOT to copy them) than in carelessness regarding such things" ("A Retrospect" 13). With this background in and belief regarding meter, Pound's inclusion of an epigraph at the beginning of *Des Imagistes* that alludes to Bion—the poet he would later claim as an expert on meter—seems to reinforce the argument that from the outset Pound constructed *Des Imagistes* to present the origins and attributes of Imagist practice rather than theorize them. In the case of this opening epigraph, Pound seems to point towards the fact that the Imagists had studied and understood poetic tradition, and their use of free verse did not break from it as much as reestablish the best of its practices by building from and merging them with more modern approaches.

Following that epigraph, Pound continues his effort to provide a defining rhetoric for Imagism through the implicit associations created by his arrangement of the poems and poets in *Des Imagistes*. Again, Nichols broaches this topic by stating, "*Des Imagistes* juxtaposes poems that thematize the clashing of poetic traditions . . . or exhibit new styles. In effect, the anthology foregrounds the processes by which new poetry emerges from prior literary traditions, specifically poetry that demands new reading habits." To support his point, Nichols discusses the Imagists' prevalent use of Greek themes and Pound's "imitations of Chinese poetry" (177). Despite his excellent assessment of Pound's movement from Greek to Asian subjects, Nichols finds a "clash" of traditions or an "exhibition of new styles" where I see an amalgamation of poetic approaches, ancient and modern.

To illustrate the clash of traditions, Nichols cites "Richard Aldington's 'Choricus' [*sic*] [as] boldly announc[ing] a break with the past with the opening line, 'The ancient songs / Pass deathward mournfully'" (177). Rather than read this poem as reveling in or glorifying a contemporary approach to poetry that leaves classical modes on the brink of extinction, I understand it as mourning the loss of the ancient traditions that have fallen into desuetude. In fact, I believe that Aldington, in an act of solidarity, subtly uses his punctuation to transform his work from a comment on the loss of "the ancient songs" into one of those ancient songs itself. This transition occurs in the fifth full stanza and reads:

> And of all the ancient songs
> Passing to the swallow blue halls
> By the dark streams of Persephone,
> This only remains:
> That we turn to thee,
> Death,
> That we turn to thee, singing
> One last song. (8)

By including a colon after the first four lines of this stanza, which begins with "of all ancient songs" and ends with "This only remains," Aldington changes his poem from a consideration of the mortality of ancient songs into a mimetic embodiment of its subject, wherein its speaker joins the chorus and the poem becomes the last of their songs. With this transition of perspective and purpose, Aldington creates a space within his poem that allows his speaker to step outside of common temporal restrictions and present his or her subject from both a modern and ancient point of reference. Far from representing a clash of traditions, then, this poem demonstrates a merging of perspectives and technique based on a similarity of design and intent.

After his discussion of "Choricos," Nichols asserts that "subsequent poems by Aldington, HD [*sic*], F. S. Flint, Amy Lowell, and William Carlos Williams complicate the dismissal of classical poetic tradition by taking Grecian topics as their themes." He continues, however, by stating that "those themes are updated as they are rendered in free verse, suggesting that imagism's primary focus is reinventing the past for a modern audience" (177). Even though I do not find anything particularly Greek about Flint and Lowell's poems in *Des Imagistes*, I believe that when Nichols attributes the use of free verse in *Des Imagistes* to the Imagists' "primary focus" of "reinventing the past," he not only underestimates the many other ways, besides free verse, in which Symbolism and Impressionism influenced Imagist practice (topics I will examine in more detail later), but also fails to recognize that by merging those ancient and modern sources the Imagists create a brand of poetry neither classical nor avant-garde, but one that produces for its readers a "sudden sense of liberation" because it remains "free from time limits and space limits" (Pound, "A Few Don'ts" 200). Furthermore, by claiming that the Imagists' use of free verse "updated" the Greek themes of their poetry, Nichols also overlooks the fact that both H.D. and Aldington developed their brands of free verse not from a modern impulse, but out of their study of classical Greek poetry.[2] Rather than viewing the Imagism Pound presents in *Des Imagistes* as arising out of either a conflict between multiple poetic traditions or a dissolution of the past, I uphold that Pound's choice of poems and their arrangement in that anthology offers a presentation of Imagism that positions itself "in accordance with the best tradition, as they found it in the best writers of all time" (Flint, "Imagisme" 136),[3] which includes modern French Symbolism and literary Impressionism along with its ancient Greek and Asian influences.

Following the first two poems, "Choricos" and "To a Greek Marble," which instantly align the anthology with Greek poetics, Aldington's third piece, "Au Vieux Jardin," takes a French title like the anthology itself, and with its mentioning of "water lilies" and the color "rose" (11), it could also allude to Baudelaire and his *Fleurs du Mal*. Because Aldington's poems return to their Greek themes after this piece and are reinforced by the "straight Greek" of H.D.'s work that follows them, Pound's inclusion and placement of "Au Vieux Jardin" cleverly reestablishes an associational hint of Symbolism within Imagist practice that does not detract from its originality, but instead presents Imagism as emerging out of a confluence of Greek and Symbolist poetics.

After H.D., Pound continues his anthology with the work of F. S. Flint. Whereas H.D.'s poetry further establishes the Imagist's affiliation with ancient Greece, Flint's section begins with a poem that returns the readers of *Des Imagistes* to his contemporary London. While this shift in geographic and temporal contexts reasserts Imagism's status as a poetic method forged and able to assimilate traits from disparate poetic traditions, Flint's poem "The Swan," which concludes his work in the anthology, also draws from and strengthens the connection between Imagism and Symbolism with its choice of topic.

Having begun to champion French Symbolism in his reviews for the *New Age* in 1908 and then authoring an extensive survey of that poetic movement for *Poetry Review* in August 1912, Flint was certainly aware that both Baudelaire's "Le Cygne" and Mallarmé's "Le vierge, le vivace et le bel aujourd'hui" have a swan as their subject and central symbol. By also choosing a swan for the subject of his poem, Flint not only recognizes and alludes to his Symbolist predecessors, but also uses his technique to strengthen their association with Imagism by initially presenting his swan through the "laconic speech of the Imagistes" (Pound, *Selected Letters* 177):

> Over the green cold leaves
> and the rippled silver
> and the tarnished copper
> of its neck and beak,
> toward the deep black water
> beneath the arches,
> the swan floats slowly.

And then as an ephemeral symbol:

> Into the dark of the arch the swan floats
> and into the black depth of my sorrow
> it bears a white rose of flame. (35)

One could view this confluence of poetic approaches as diluting the Imagist integrity of the piece. But if one accepts Pound's articulation of the "one-image poem" as a type of "super-position" or "one idea set on top of another" ("Vorticism" 286), then it is possible to view Flint as creating an Image in this section of his poem by layering his Imagist presentation of the swan "on top" of his personal and Symbolist interpretation of that bird. By deciding to include this work in *Des Imagistes* and use it as the last of

Flint's offerings, Pound directly speaks to the degree of influence that he (and Flint) believes Symbolism had on Imagist practice, as well as to how much he thinks Imagism might benefit from the association. Moreover, by creating an Image that includes a symbol within its structural makeup, Flint offers a poetic sequence that not only literally enacts the process of Imagism growing out of the Symbolist impulse, but also provides a locus point that demonstrates both the similarities and differences between those two different approaches to poetry.

After Flint, Pound includes three poems by three different authors—Skipwith Cannell, Amy Lowell, and William Carlos Williams—poems that with their use of free verse and direct presentation of their subjects demonstrate strength in or reinforce at least two aspects of Pound's Imagist program. Prior to this grouping, Pound arranges his anthology in such a manner as to allow the work of Imagism's main practitioners to identify the origins and principles of that poetic practice, but with this group he showcases the effects that Imagism can have upon the work of writers less notably associated with Imagism and/or still in the early stages of their careers. Each of these writers had already come under his sphere of influence in one way or another. By including their work in *Des Imagistes*, Pound could not only help accelerate their careers and broaden his own Imagist net to provide variation within his anthology, but also present works that did not bear traces of the classical and French influences upon Imagism so much as highlight the consolidated influence of Imagism itself.

Although Pound incorporates James Joyce's "I Hear an Army" as the next poem in *Des Imagistes* to help promote Joyce's literary career as well, the presence of that work also makes another implicit argument regarding the Imagists' use of free verse. In his poem, Joyce, in the typical Imagist manner, focuses on the direct treatment of his subject but, unlike the other poets in the anthology, writes his poem according to a complex metrical form.[4] Much like his allusion to Bion, then, Pound uses Joyce's poem to demonstrate that Imagism does not require the use of free verse as much as it positions the Imagist poet's mission as identifying and utilizing the form that best expresses the subject of his or her poem, whether it be in free verse or not.

Interestingly, political considerations seem to have weighed as heavily as poetic technique in Pound's decisions to include many of the poets in *Des Imagistes*. Widely regarded as a tireless promoter of other writers as well as a literary impresario, Pound frequently helped those whose work he admired to find publication. As a self-appointed arbiter of taste, however, Pound endorsed writers who tended to share, or demonstrate sympathies with, his own aesthetic predispositions. Hence, and as Robert Frost took pains to acknowledge,[5] much of the effort Pound expended on others also solidified his own literary position and convictions. Nowhere is this dual-purposed agenda of Pound's more prevalent in *Des Imagistes* than with this grouping of poets that begins with Cannell and ends with Joyce. Pound had a specific reason to include each of these writers beyond simply the merit of their poetry: Cannell was also an American poet experimenting with free verse who came to England by way of Philadelphia; Lowell had already fully committed herself to becoming an Imagist, and her wealth and social background could certainly assist a fledging poetic movement; Williams was a friend and artistic confidant of Pound's since their time together at the University of Pennsylvania; and Joyce had been recommended by Pound's most notable literary connection, William Butler Yeats. To think that Pound chose these or any of the other writers to appear in *Des Imagistes* based solely on personal or political reasons, however, would be a mistake. Rather, Pound selected authors whose work contained elements of his concept of Imagism, whether they represented the past, present, or future of the burgeoning movement. The fact that he maintained personal relationships with many of the contributors only suggests that they had the opportunity to influence, or be influenced by, Pound and his concept of Imagism, and therefore, by that link primarily, they merited inclusion in the anthology representing Imagist practice.

Because of their different relationships to that practice, and the fact that they precede Pound's own contributions to *Des Imagistes*, the poems by Cannell, Lowell, Williams, and Joyce also offer something of a palate cleanser before the main course of Pound himself. Yet despite the ways in which this arrangement draws attention to Pound and his poetry, it also expertly anticipates the need to reassert those core attributes of Imagism established earlier in the anthology before complicating them through the introduction of new ones. In his own section, Pound begins by returning to the Greek in his first two poems before including four epigrammatic reworkings of texts he found in Herbert Giles's *History of Chinese Literature* (Carpenter 222). Through this ordering, Pound immediately reestablishes the dominant theme of the Greek influence on Imagism, which begins with the anthology's opening epigraph and continues through the poetry of Aldington and H.D., before he introduces the presence of an Asian aesthetic that also plays a primary role in his concept of Imagist poetics—a role that becomes more prevalent than the Greek in the poems following Pound's. By placing and arranging his poems in the anthology as he does, Pound allows them to operate as a transitive regrouping point that both reaffirms and complicates those influences and techniques that define Imagism for him. Moreover, Pound's section in *Des Imagistes* also marks the dividing line in the anthology between those artists whose work he and his Imagist agenda influenced and those whose work influenced him and his development of that agenda.

Fittingly, then, after his own poetry, Pound inserts the single longest piece of the collection, Ford Madox Hueffer's "In the Little Old Market-Place." Despite the fact that neither Pound nor Hueffer himself ever considered his poetry to be fully "Imagist," they both understood his influential role in shaping the practices of that school. In his 1913 article "Status Rerum," Pound states that he "would rather talk about poetry with Ford Madox Hueffer than with any man in London," and that "Mr. Hueffer believes in an exact rendering of things. He would strip words of all 'association' for the sake of getting a precise meaning. . . . He is objective" (125). Then, after praising the same Hueffer poem that he would later include in *Des Imagistes*, Pound, possibly signaling the influence of Hueffer, shifts directly, if not abruptly, into a discussion of the Imagists. For his part, Hueffer states in the foreword to the *Imagist Anthology 1930*, entitled "Those Were the Days," that he would "like to think that [his] ceaseless hammerings . . . had their effect on the promoters of [Imagism]," and that he "considered" the Imagists as "writers perfectly calculated to carry on the work that [he] had, not so much begun, as tried to foster in others" (Ford 18).

In "Status Rerum," Pound cautions his reader that Impressionism "tends to lapse into description" (125), and he seems to distinguish its style from Imagism by stating, in a review of Hueffer's *High Germany*, "Impressionism belongs in paint, it is of the eye. . . . Poetry is in some odd way concerned with the specific gravity of things, with their nature," as well as by arguing that "the *conception* of poetry is a process more intense than the *reception* of an impression. And no impression, however carefully articulated, can, recorded, convey that feeling of sudden light which the work of art should and must convey" ("Book of the Month" 133).[6] Nevertheless, he certainly comprehended and valued the influence that Hueffer and Impressionism had on him and his development of the Imagist program. Therefore, despite that Hueffer's poem tends to describe more than present and, thereby, registers Impressions rather than objective Images, Pound's decision to include it in *Des Imagistes*, once again, marks his willingness to recognize and define Imagism through the presence of its influences.

Finally, Pound concludes the main body of *Des Imagistes* with Allen Upward's "Scented Leaves from a Chinese Jar" and John Cournos's "The Rose." Interestingly, it was Upward's poem, which appeared in *Poetry* in September 1913, that sparked Pound's interest in Chinese Literature, and it was also Upward, once the two met, who introduced Pound to Giles's *History of Chinese Literature* (Carr 601-04). By deciding to place Upward's poem after his own, and as one of the last two pieces in the anthology, Pound reiterates the influence of Asian literature upon Imagism that he first signaled with his own poetry, while also creating the impression that his familiarity with that aesthetic precedes and supersedes Upward's.

While Upward's poem supports the presentation of Imagism as a poetic movement aligned with and containing traits of Asian poetics, Cournos's poem demonstrates that Imagism not only adopts the best practices from the best traditions, but also improves upon those texts by then reapplying its own hybridized poetic method back upon them. In "The Rose," Cournos, in a manner similar to that of Aldington, H.D., and Pound, rewrites a poem originally written in a foreign language—in this case, Polish—to highlight and emphasize its own intrinsic Imagist traits. Through this transference of technique, however, Cournos, like those other Imagists, illustrates that Imagism exists not as a poetic method built upon the clashing of varied traditions, but as one that utilizes a symbiotic relationship with its influences to produce original works neither derivative nor without literary precedent.

Ultimately, one finds that as editor of *Des Imagistes* Pound manipulates the order, arrangement, and allusive potentials of the works he includes within his anthology so as to offer an Image of Imagism itself. Much like his later concept of super-positioning, which places one idea on top of another in order to create an Image, Pound organizes the poems and poets in *Des Imagistes* in such a manner that their similarities and differences simultaneously reveal and reinforce the defining aspects of his Imagist program. Furthermore, with that arrangement, Pound obliquely acknowledges the origins of and influences on Imagism, both ancient and modern, not only to generate interest in his collection, but also to demonstrate that, as a poetic program, Imagism operates as a confluence of the best poetic techniques, wherein each melds into a single, direct, and precise poetic effort—or that, even prior to its eventual name change, his concept of Imagist practice already existed as a "Vortex."

## Notes

1. Aldington's "The Mourning for Bion" first appeared in *The New Freewoman* (1913).

2. H.D. took as her first poetic models the Greek poet Theocritus and the works included in J. W. Mackail's 1890 collection, *Select Epigrams from the Greek Anthology*. In comparing H.D.'s "Hermes of the Ways" with its source, an epigram by Anyte of Tegea, Helen Carr states, "H.D.'s poem is longer, more developed than the original, as is often the case in her translations, yet the effect sounds as spare as a faithful translation from the Greek" (493). Barbara Guest also asserts that "With the instinct of sudden genius, [H.D.] recognized the form that suited her sensibility, and that form proceeded from Greek drama and Greek poetry" (44).

    Furthermore, Aldington wrote in a letter to Amy Lowell, dated November 1917:

> "I began to write vers libre about the early part of 1911, partly because I was fatigued with rhyme and partly because of the interest I had in poetic experiment. I didn't know Heine or Patmore's 'Unknown Eros' & never suspected the existence of the French vers libristes. I got the idea from a chorus in the Hippolytus of Euripides. In fact the cadence of Choricos and the Greek Marble . . . is very similar to that of Hippolytus' invocation to Artemis, though, of course, the subject is very different" (*An Autobiography* 28).

3. Although this essay is attributed to Flint's authorship in the March 1913 issue of *Poetry*, Pound mentions in a letter to Dorothy Shakespear that Flint wrote it "chiefly at my own dictation" (*Ezra Pound and Dorothy Shakespear* 179).

4. Layeh Bock states that Joyce's poem "is cast in a complex pattern of alternating duple and triple feet, and follows patterns of rhyme and assonance" (231).

5. In her book *The Verse Revolutionaries*, Helen Carr characterizes Robert Frost as "the most bitter and resentful recipient of [Pound's] assistance" (595). Also, Lawrance Thompson, in his three-volume biography of the New England poet, includes a poem that Frost wrote and sent to F. S. Flint in which Frost suggests that Pound only helped him in order to improve his own literary standing (*The Early Years* 421-23). Thompson additionally quotes Frost as later referring to Pound's efforts to help younger poets, such as himself, as "selfish generosity" (*The Later Years* 223).

6. Even though Pound does not specifically mention Imagism as the particular type of poetry that he sets in opposition to Impressionism in his review of *High Germany*, the "odd way" that he perceives that poetry as addressing the nature of things seems to presage his later definition of the Image in "A Few Don'ts by an Imagiste" as "that which presents an intellectual and emotional complex in an instant of time." Additionally, his foregrounding of the "conception" of poetry also aligns with his remarks regarding Imagist technique that follow that definition, as does his description of the "feeling of sudden light," which sounds strikingly similar to the "sense of sudden liberation" and/or "sudden growth" that he attributes to the Imagist "complex" in that same article (200).

## Works Cited

Aldington, Richard. *An Autobiography in Letters*. Ed. Norman T. Gates. University Park: Pennsylvania State UP. 1992. Print.

---. "The Mourning for Bion." *The New Freewoman* 15 September 1913: 133. Print.

Bock, Layeh Aronson. *The Birth of Modernism: "Des Imagistes" and the Psychology of William James*. Diss. Stanford U, 1980. Ann Arbor: UMI, 1981. Print.

Carpenter, Humphrey. *A Serious Character: The Life of Ezra Pound*. Boston: Houghton Mifflin, 1988. Print.

Carr, Helen. *The Verse Revolutionaries: Ezra Pound, H.D. and the Imagists*. London: Random House, 2009. Print.

Eliot, T. S. "Ezra Pound: His Metric and Poetry." *To Criticize the Critic and Other Writings*. Lincoln: U of Nebraska P, 1991. 162-82. Print.

Flint, Frank Stewart. "Imagisme." *Poetry* 1.6 (1913): 198-200. Print.

---. *The Fourth Imagist: Selected Poems of F. S. Flint*. Ed. Michael Copp. Cranbury, NJ: Rosemont Publishing, 2007. Print.

Ford, Ford Madox. "Those Were the Days." *Imagist Anthology 1930*. Ed. Richard Aldington. New York: Covici, Friede, 1930. 13-21. Print.

Guest, Barbara. *Herself Defined: H.D. and her World*. Tucson, AZ: Schaffner, 2003. Print.

Nichols, John G. "Ezra Pound's Poetic Anthologies and the Architecture of Reading." *PMLA* 121 (2006): 170-85. Print.

Pound, Ezra. "Book of the Month." *Poetry Review* 1.3 (1912): 133. Print.

---, ed. *Des Imagistes: An Anthology*. New York: Albert and Charles Boni, 1914. Print.

---. *Ezra Pound: Selected Prose 1909 - 1965*. Ed. William Cookson. New York: New Directions, 1973. Print.

---. "A Few Don'ts by an Imagiste." *Poetry* 1.6 (1913): 200-01. Print.

---. "A Retrospect." *Literary Essays of Ezra Pound*. Ed. T. S. Eliot. New York:

New Directions, 1935. 3-14. Print.

---. *The Selected Letters of Ezra Pound: 1907 - 1941*. Ed. D. D. Paige. New York: New Directions, 1971. Print.

---. "Status Rerum." *Poetry* 1.4 (1913): 123-27. Print.

---. "Vorticism." *Early Writings: Poems and Prose*. Ed. Ira B. Nadel. New York: Penguin Books, 2005. 278-91. Print.

Pound, Ezra, and Dorothy Shakespear. *Ezra Pound and Dorothy Shakespear: Their Letters: 1909-1914*. Ed. Omar Pound and A. Walton Litz. New York: New Directions, 1984. Print.

Thompson, Lawrance. *Robert Frost: The Early Years, 1874-1915*. New York: Holt, 1966. Print.

Thompson, Lawrance, and R. H. Winnick. *Robert Frost: The Later Years, 1938-1963*. New York: Holt, 1976. Print.

# "I cling to the spar":
# Imagism in Ezra Pound's Vortex

Critical attention to the intersections between Imagism and Vorticism has long mapped a smooth transition from one aesthetic experiment to the other. In *The Pound Era*, Hugh Kenner asserts that "the Image became the Vortex" (161). Yet it is also clear that he sees Imagism as a lesser forerunner of the "Great English Vortex." Imagism was "invented to launch H.D.," Kenner notes, but for Pound it "soon entailed negotiating with dim and petulant people: Fletcher, say, or Flint, or Aldington, and eventually Miss Lowell" (191).[1] A harsher putdown of *Les Imagistes* is hard to imagine. I contend, however, that far from disowning the Imagist project, as Kenner alleges, Pound's collaboration with Vorticists, including Wyndham Lewis, Henri Gaudier-Brzeska, Ford Madox Ford (then Hueffer), and Jessie Dismorr, among others, was informed by a strong residual Imagism, which he would never quite let go of. Nor would Vorticists write off Imagists out of hand. For among the signatories of the Vorticist "Manifesto" in *Blast* (1915), the movement's polemical little magazine, we find a prime mover of Imagism, Richard Aldington. This might come as a surprise at first. A closer look at the "Manifesto," however, uncovers traces of the Imagist aesthetic in its tribute to "bareness and hardness" (Aldington *et al.* 41). In a classic illustration of the hybridity of modernism, both movements also promoted a philosophy of art inimical to the Romantics, the "great enemies" of the London Vortex. Moreover, Imagists and Vorticists alike balked at the Futurists. The Italian movement's "gush over machines, aeroplanes, etc." rendered Futurists "the most romantic and sentimental 'moderns' to be found" (Aldington *et al.* 41). Aldington would continue to associate with Vorticists as Assistant Editor of *The Egoist*, and beyond it.[2] My discussion subscribes to the idea put forth by T. S. Eliot—himself a one-time contributor to *Blast*—that Imagism may be seen as "the starting-point of modern poetry" (*To Criticize the Critic* 58). As for Pound, the minimalist poetic experiment would become a defining matrix for his art.

Wallace Stevens is not a poet typically associated with Imagism. Yet in an essay on William Carlos Williams, he inadvertently sheds light on the Imagist legacy in Pound's poetry and aesthetic philosophy. "Imagism is not something superficial," Stevens insists, "It obeys an instinct. Moreover, imagism is an ancient phase of poetry. It is something permanent" (258). My purpose is to investigate the extent to which Pound continues to heed the Imagist "instinct" in his Vorticist phase. I seek to track Imagist principles that may further inform, and perhaps complicate, our reading of Pound's investment in the Vorticist project. To this end, I will discuss the Imagist register in brief close readings of selected poems published primarily in *Blast*'s "War Issue" of 1915.[3]

Perhaps nowhere else is the kinship between Imagism and Pound's Vorticism more in evidence than in his oft-quoted aphorism published in *Poetry* in March 1913, "An Image is that which presents an intellectual and emotional complex in an instant of time" (*Literary Essays* 4). It is reprinted verbatim in *Blast* 1 under the heading "Ancestry" ("Vortex" 154). Sharing the same "ancestral" space are Pater, Whistler, Picasso, and Kandinsky. Pound thus situates the semiotics of Imagism in tandem with the interdisciplinary art-historical writing of the Vortex. The stylistic economy of Pound's Imagist slogan also informs his Vorticist doctrine of "The Primary Pigment," which holds that "every concept, every emotion presents itself to the vivid consciousness in some primary form. It belongs to the art of this form" ("Vortex" 154). It is not far-fetched, I think, to see the Vorticist saying as a dialectical turn on the Imagist saying, with the Vorticist postscript—"It belongs to the art of this form"—rendering it inclusive of all the arts. Pound's definition of the Image also inflects his key Vorticist concept of "The Turbine," a vortex that swallows all experience and "all the energized past" ("Vortex" 153). The cognitive-experiential compression of time encoded here would be integral to the movement's radical aesthetics. The "sense of sudden liberation" Pound had proposed in 1912 in "A Few Don'ts by an Imagiste" (*Literary Essays* 4) may simply have found in the vortical image a new form of technological primitivism, designed in part to undercut the mechanistic fetishism of Futurist poetics. More important, his willful synthesis of Imagist and Vorticist principles would continue to underpin his poetry and prose long after his formal association with both experiments.

Pound steadfastly sought to create a style of verse "as much like granite as it can be," as he phrases it even as late as 1917 (*Literary Essays* 12). This purview arguably shares closer affinity with Imagist accentual *vers libre* than with the militant poetics and machine-form aesthetic of Vorticism. Poetry, he famously affirms, ought to be "austere, direct, free from emotional slither." Eileen Gregory associates this classicist directness with "an ascetic ideal" in Pound and H.D. (17). Though Pound's verse would alternate between stark and wildly allusive, in the early nineteen teens he still upheld a rather austere, lean poetic aesthetic. In a letter to Amy Lowell of 1 August 1914, just a few months after the publication of the anthology *Des Imagistes* in February, he writes, "Imagism stands, or I should like it to stand for hard, light, clear edges" (*Selected Letters* 38).[4]

In a fascinating twist Pound prints H.D.'s Imagist poem "Oread" (then untitled) in *Blast* 1 as a "primary pigment" or "primary expression" of Vorticist verse ("Vortex" 154). Even more astonishing to anyone accustomed to thinking of H.D.'s poetry as wholly Imagist is the fact that Pound explicitly likens the poem to Kandinsky's and Picasso's prodigious feats in painting. Incidentally, Lowell would also include H.D.'s poem (with its present title) in her own anthology of 1915, *Some Imagist Poets*. Yet Pound's editorial gambit in *Blast* 1 presages his scorn for Lowell's ersatz version of Imagism, "Amygism."[5] Where David Moody believes that Pound cites "Oread" in *Blast* as "the exemplary *Imagiste* poem" (226), I would contend that the poet showcases it as a Vorticist specimen, if only to collapse the arbitrary boundaries between both movements. H.D.'s tightly-controlled piece reads:

Whirl up sea —
Whirl your pointed pines,
Splash your great pines

On our rocks,
Hurl your green over us,
Cover us with your pools of fir. (154)

Susan Stanford Friedman has perceptively characterized the poem as
"phenomenological," that is, a poem "about consciousness, not the world of
objects external to consciousness" (56). So described, the poem uncannily
instantiates Lewis's saying in *Blast* 1, "Reality is in the artist, the image
only in life" ("Futurism" 135). In his turn, by giving H.D's poem pride of
place in *Blast* 1 under the heading "Poetry," Pound seems keen to show
that even textbook Imagist verse can defy programmatic submission to
style or, as he puts it, "mimicry" ("Vortex" 154). It is also possible that
he may have been drawn to the proto-Vorticist stirrings in the poem's
spiral imagery and imperative mood. The gyral verb, "whirl," in the two-
line anaphora at the start provides a sharp contrast to the "splash" that
joyously weds the "whirled up" sea and the "pointed pines" within the
mountain-nymph's consciousness. The poem effectively combines the
lyrical terseness of Imagism and the pictorial syncretism of Vorticism. For
Pound, the "primary pigment of poetry" embedded in H.D's mythopoeic
image explicitly illustrates the "primary media" (namely, "direct treatment
of the 'thing'"[6]) and "primary expression" (namely, "to use absolutely no
word that does not contribute to the presentation") which would inform
both aesthetic experiments.

In *Gaudier-Brzeska, A Memoir* (1916), Pound cautions critics against
reading too much into labels such as Vorticism:

> At no time was it intended that either Mr. Lewis, or Gaudier
> or myself or Mr. Wadsworth or Mr. Etchells should crawl into
> each other's skins or that we should in any way surrender our
> various identities, or that the workings of certain fundamental
> principles of *the arts* should force any one of us to turn his own
> particular *art* into a flat imitation of the external features of the
> particular art of any other member of our group. (25, Pound's
> emphasis)

The phrase "the workings of certain fundamental principles of *the arts*" may
help to explain the ebb and flow of Imagist values in Pound's alliance with

the Vorticists, while the excerpt as a whole betrays anxiety about individual expression and in-group collectivism. Pound's blunt refusal to "surrender" his own artistic identity to the trans-aesthetic of the Vorticist brand (or any other brand, for that matter) suggests that he never cast off the poetic primacy that Imagism afforded. That is also to say that his Imagist phase itself evolved, finding a local habitation and a name in Vorticism. I do not mean to suggest, of course, that Pound's Vorticism amounts to nothing more than a revved-up version of Imagism. If anything, Vorticist heterodoxy in the arts *assimilated* the prosodic tenets of Imagism. But where Vorticism would serve as a vehicle with which to engage a wider range of the arts, Imagism would still retain for Pound a stripped-down poetic economy with which to offset "delicate and exhausted metres" ("Fratres Minores") in contemporary French and Anglophone poetry.[7]

Among the motley crew of Vorticists Pound may be seen as the odd poet out. Lewis's editorial for *Blast* 2 acknowledges that the magazine "is run chiefly *by* Painters and *for* Painting" ("Notice to Public," my emphasis). Following her performative definition of Imagism—"to present an image"— Lowell openly challenges this aspect of Vorticism in her preface to *Some Imagist Poets*, saying: "We are not a school of painters" (vii). Keenly aware of this painterly-pictorial bias in the Vortex, Pound strives to fit in. It is little wonder, then, that the first poem in *Blast* 2, "Dogmatic Statement on the Game and Play of Chess," is subtitled "(Theme for a Series of Pictures)." Pound's Imagist credo to "use no superfluous word, no adjective which does not reveal something" (*Literary Essays* 4) is put to the test in the very first line: "Red knights, brown bishops, bright queens." The image is paratactic, that is to say, non-discursively expressive. It is also playfully subversive, a kitschy revamping of traditionally monochromatic chess pieces. The poem syntactically weds the function of each piece to color and light. The red knights lead the charge, "falling in strong 'L's' of colour." The kinetic, alliterative energy of the opening line climaxes in the pieces "Striking the board . . . / Reaching and striking in angles, / Holding lines of one colour:"[.] The colon after "colour" holds in abeyance the energy of the trope. This is a game of chess as expressionist painting, à la Kandinsky. The poem turns on a Neoplatonic apotheosis: "This board is alive with light / These pieces are living in form."

The change in visual register—the inanimate board turned animate— seems to unfold precisely along the same phenomenological lines (in

Friedman's sense) as Pound's explanation for his "*hokku*-like" poem "In a Station of the Metro," in which "one is trying to record the precise instant when a thing outward and objective transforms itself, or darts into a thing inward and subjective" ("Vorticism" 467). That Pound is writing about a seminal Imagist poem in a 1915 essay titled "Vorticism" bears out the reach of Imagism in his poetic ken. The "terseness and intensity of imagery" (77) that Yoshinobu Hakutani deems critical to Pound's interest in the Japanese poetic form convey precisely the virtues that made Imagism so vital for him. As Andrew Thacker points out, "included at the centre of Imagist 'newness' was not only the temporally outdated, whether in Aldington and H.D.'s Hellenicism or Pound's Provence, but also the geographically distant" (42). Seen in this light, even his Vorticist meditation on chess—as it happens, a game of Asian origin—appears closer in praxis to Imagism. Its "hard, light, clear edges" (*Selected Letters* 38) reify Pound's belief in "'absolute rhythm,' a rhythm, that is, in poetry which corresponds exactly to the emotion or shade of emotion to be expressed" (*Literary Essays* 9). I would suggest that the poem attempts to convey the exact "emotion" of apprehending a game of chess in its totality. The sheer play of images is held together by a creative tension between submission to the rules of the game (knights must trace "strong 'L's'") and the freedom to renew tradition, as the movements of chess pieces on the board "break and reform the pattern." Again, this is precisely what Pound describes in the Imagist manifesto as "that sense of sudden liberation" (*Literary Essays* 4).

Yet the poem also contains one of his most nakedly Vorticist poetic pronouncements. With echoes of H.D.'s anaphoric "whirl" in "Oread," it caps a sequence of moves in which the "Luminous green from the rooks" clashes with the

> . . . "x's" of queens,
> Looped with the knight-leaps.
> "Y" pawns, cleaving, embanking,
> Whirl, centripetal, mate, King down in the vortex:
> Clash, leaping of bands, straight strips of hard colours,
> Blocked lights working in, escapes, renewing of contes[.]

The deliberate absence of a full stop at the end, following "contes" (a French word for "tales" or "stories" but also suggesting "contest" for Pound), may signify the Vorticist polylingual commitment to "renew,"—or "make it new," in Pound's celebrated phrase—the art and culture of its time. The poem's overdetermined semiotics appears to combine at a stroke the main media of Vorticist expression (poetry, painting, sculpture, and prose) to "checkmate" its aesthetic rivals. Even so, these verses still exhibit Hulmean-Imagist traces, as I have suggested.[8] Further evidence of this imagistic strain follows from Michael H. Whitworth's notion of the apparent absence of causality in Imagist poetry, leaving the reader "to determine whether relations of similarity or causation are being proposed" (46). Accordingly, although the chess pieces are not, strictly speaking, anthropomorphized, they nonetheless seem self-propelled: "Their moves break and reform the pattern." The poem images the cognitive experience of a game of chess, but without the artifice of a unifying conscience or observer. In contrast, the more rigorously Vorticist poems often privilege causal-connective impressions, as in Jessie Dismorr's "Monologue": "I ache all over, but acrobatic, I undertake the feat of existence / Details of equipment delight me." It is no wonder that Lewis grew wary of the way Pound "stretched" Vorticism (Materer 231).

Pound's supposedly fraught Vorticism may be less puzzling if we situate Imagism as the "first anti-avant-garde," to quote Lawrence Rainey (30). To Rainey's well-warranted view that Imagism "shunned the kind of programmatic ambitions associated with Futurism," I would offer that Vorticism also comes to seem programmatic, especially in its manifestic slogans, "blasts," and "blesses." In contrast, the Imagist ethos held that the movement constitutes "only a poetic school, devoted to study, craft and tradition" (Peppis 32). In my reading, Pound continued to draw from his doctrine of the image even as he freely experimented with Vorticism. In one of the first sustained studies of the movement, Glenn Hughes recounts a conversation with Pound in which the poet explains that in writing the Imagist manifesto "he was guided by a desire to formulate the points of agreement between the various imagist poets. The manifesto was not, could not be, an expression of the individualities of the poets" (29). The endgame for Pound is to explore poetic possibilities and cultivate aesthetic autonomy beyond the confines of poetic prescriptions, even his own.

In "I Gather the Limbs of Osiris" (1911), Pound presents the "luminous detail" as a tool to "clear up a certain messy place in the history of literature" (*Selected Prose* 23). With proto-Imagist undertones, he says that the "artist

seeks out the luminous detail and presents it. He does not comment" (23).
Pound's paratactic technique often produces more heat than light, as the
more baffling passages in *The Cantos* evince. All the same, this mode of
procedure may serve to illustrate how Imagism continued to keep his
poetry lean yet complex—a "cubist surface," as Marjorie Perloff has dubbed
*The Cantos* (182).

"Et Faim Sallir Le Loup Des Boys," Pound's last poem in *Blast* 2, arguably
manifests even more striking Imagist properties. With its stoic nod to the
travails of life at sea, the opening lines bring to mind the "ice-cold sea" of
his 1911 translation of the Anglo-Saxon poem "The Seafarer." The *Blast*
poem, however, exhibits the "fiercely anti-bourgeois" (Alexander 76) tenor
of the eighth-century poem even more pointedly:

> I cling to the spar,
> Washed with the cold salt ice
> I cling to the spar.

While much of Vorticist art is a commentary on the machine age, the
starkness of this image telegraphs Pound's imagistic asceticism. It might not
be too far-fetched to interpret "spar" (a ship's mast) as a sly pun on "spare"
(in the sense of "sparse"). Seen thus, the image conveys the poet's "clinging"
to poetic essentials, essentials that steer his verse back into Imagist waters.
In the fourth line, the image of a poet-hero besieged by "insidious modern
waves, civilization, civilized hidden snares" typifies Aldington's blueprint
for modern poetry. Published in *The Egoist* in May 1915—just two months
prior to the publication of *Blast* 2—it prescribes

> ... an escape from artificiality and sentimentality in poetry, and
> that is by rendering the moods, the emotions, the impressions
> of a single, sensitized personality confronted by the phenomena
> of modern life, and by expressing these moods accurately, in
> concrete, precise, racy language. (Aldington 80)

Pound's poem duly goes on to defend his Vorticist friends against "cowardly
editors," who become the target of as racy an epithet as ever: "Merde!" ("Et
Faim"). He probably has in mind, among others, his editor at the *New
Age*, Alfred Orage. Under the alias "R.H.C.," Orage had called Imagism

"nonsense" and "rubbish without hope" in the 8 October 1914 issue of the weekly review (549). That same month, George Prothero, "the editor of the prestigious *Quarterly Review*, which Pound had been cultivating since 1912, had rejected his proposals for further contributions, on the basis of his affiliation with *Blast*" (Beasley 115). Just as Pound had refused to "sing their cant" ("Et Faim"), so, too, he would play loose with Vorticism itself. His tense relationship with the London Vortex may indeed have informed the elegiac, dirge-like end of his 1915 poem: "Friends fall off at the pinch, the loveliest die. / That is the path of life, this is my forest" ("Et Faim"). While the allusion to the War is inescapable, I would also suggest a less literal reading in which Pound, like the titular hungry wolf coming out of the woods, acts out what Lyotard describes as the "civil war of language" (141).

In blurring the boundaries of Image and Vortex in *Blast*, Pound may have been trying to resist being swallowed up in the geometrical-abstract style of Vorticism. The young Gauguinesque poet he mocks in the footnote to another poem in *Blast* 2, "Our Contemporaries," shows the pitfalls of cultish allegiance to a collectivist aesthetic: "ses poèmes sont remplis seulement de ses propres subjectivités, style Victorienne de la 'Georgian Anthology.'"[9] Pound's anti-Georgian ethos seems merely to parrot Vorticist propaganda. Yet his thematic concerns in other poems in *Blast* suggest that his allegiance to the Vorticist avant-garde is dubious at best. Even a cursory glance at these poems reveals how the ancient and the arcane hold sway in his professedly Vorticist verse. To wit, "Ancient Wisdom, rather cosmic" alludes to the Chinese Taoist philosopher, So-Shu; "Gnomic Verses" is a comical meditation on Li Po's "beautiful verses"; "Ancient Music" parodies the Middle English lyric, "Sumer Is Icumen In"; "Epitaphs" revels in drink-laden tributes to T'ang Dynasty poets, Fu I and Li Po; "Before Sleep" invokes "the gods of the underworld"; finally, "His Vision of a Certain Lady Post Mortem" describes "A brown, fat babe sitting in the lotus." Pound would reprint most of these poems in later collections, from *Lustra* (1916) to *The Cantos* (1915-1970). These references to the past seem inconsistent with the Vorticist appeal to the "Reality of the Present" ("Long Live the Vortex!" 7) and its "blessing" of England as an "Industrial Island machine" (Aldington *et al.* 23). Instead, the bulk of Pound's poems in *Blast* seems much more in keeping with the lyrical classicism of the *Des Imagistes* anthology.

In contrast, consider the metropolitan and contemporary concerns of other poets in *Blast*, from Eliot's "Preludes" and "Rhapsody of a Windy Night" and Dismorr's "London Notes" to Ford's "The Old Houses of Flanders." In "Rhapsody" Eliot typifies the Vorticist strain in the lines, "A broken spring in a factory yard / Rust that clings to the form that the strength has left / Hard and curled and ready to snap" (50). The poet's portrayal of modern detritus taps into the foundational Vorticist concept of captured energy.[10] As Murray McArthur aptly remarks, the helix-shaped spring, "thrown up by human work, is a cultural twist, a lost inanimate object mutated into the threshold of twisting itself" (515). McArthur's poststructuralist reading nonetheless misses the poem's Vorticism.[11] Consider, too, Part VI of the "Manifesto," which ends in a paean to "the forms of machinery, Factories, new and vaster buildings, bridges and works" (Aldington *et al.* 40). The Vorticism coded in "Rhapsody" can be seen right down to its final line, "The last twist of the knife" (51). While no one would seriously call Eliot a Vorticist, "Rhapsody" arguably incorporates Vorticism in a way that most of Pound's contributions to *Blast* do not. "Preludes" likewise features Vorticist experimentalism and visual abstraction, where

> His soul stretched tight across the skies
> That fade behind a city block, . . .
> I am moved by fancies that are curled
> Around these images, and cling. (49)

"Rhapsody" and "Preludes" throw into sharp relief the category-transgressing nature of Pound's poetry.

Helen Carr cogently argues that "the luminous detail is perhaps his first real move towards the doctrine of imagism, where the image's impact is instantaneous and powerful, a sudden illumination" (388). Pound's Vorticist poems, we have seen, bear out the persistence of this imagistic technique, at a time when he had apparently "moved on." The last phrase is William Wees's. In "Ezra Pound as a Vorticist," Wees assumes that because Pound's "Et Faim Sallir Le Loup Des Boys" makes no mention of H.D. or Aldington in his litany of friends—Lewis, Rodin, Epstein, Gaudier-Brzeska, and Wadsworth—"his new allegiances clearly show that he had 'moved on' from Imagism" (61). However, as I have set forth, Poundian Vorticism and Imagism intertwine in a productive tension. Pound doubtless retained Imagist principles out of a belief that poetry, to quote Hulme, "deals in images" (*Collected Writings* 55). Yet, for Pound, a concern with "explicit rendering, be it of external nature, or of emotion" may be said to trump the expediency of literary movements (*Literary Essays* 11). Many years after the War had put an end to Vorticism, the poet would bring this point home: "It took the *Manchester Guardian* or froustery six months to discover that BLAST was satirical. 24 years have not been enough to teach 'em that Vorticism was constructive. In fact, it has passed as a small local movement, and I myself do not care a hoot whether the name remains pasted to it" (*Guide to Kulchur* 266).

## Notes

1. Kenner goes so far as to say that "it is folly to pretend, in the way of historians with books to fill, that [the Imagists] were of Pound's stature. Vorticism implied his alliance with his own kind: Gaudier, Lewis" (191). Note, however, that Kenner has nothing but praise for Pound's own brand of Imagism, as it "is energy, is effort. It does not appease itself by reproducing what is seen, but by setting some other seen thing into relation" (186).

2. Aldington seems to have been particularly close to Lewis, the formidable force behind Vorticism and *Blast*, at least for a time. The friendship was no doubt strengthened by the fact that Aldington published a laudatory review of *Blast* in *The Egoist* immediately upon receiving a copy of the bombastic magazine (O'Keefe 156). Paul O'Keefe also suggests that Lewis felt comfortable enough with Aldington and his young wife to announce late in 1913, over dinner, that he had contracted Chlamydia (164).

3. All further references to *Blast* will henceforth appear as "*Blast* 1" and "*Blast* 2" to distinguish the first issue of June 1914 from the second (and final) issue of July 1915, respectively.

4. Lowell repeats Pound's call for "hard and clear" poetry in the preface to her 1915 anthology (vii).

5. See David Moody's discussion (222 ff.).

6. In *Literary Essays* (3).

7. Even the "geometric idiom" that Miranda Hickman has recently located in Vorticism seems less pronounced in Pound's own Imagistic brand of Vorticism (11).

8. I have in mind T. E. Hulme's pronouncement in "Romanticism and Classicism" that "the great aim [of classical verse] is accurate, precise and definite description" (160). In a letter to René Taupin of May 1928, Pound includes Hulme, Yeats, and the Symbolists in his genealogy of Imagism: "L'idée de l'image doit 'quelque chose' aux symbolistes français via T. E. Hulme, via Yeat[s] <Symons < Mallarmé " [*sic*] (*Selected Letters* 218).

9. The full footnote to the poem reads:

Il s'agit d'un jeune poète qui a suivi le culte de Gauguin jusqu'a Taihayti meme. Etant fort bel homme, quand la princesse bistre entendit qu'il voulait lui accorder ses faveurs elle a montré son allegresse a la manière dont nous venons de parler. Malhereusement ses poèmes sont remplis seulement de ses propres subjectivités, style Victorienne de la "Georgian Anthology." (*Blast* 2 21) This is about a young poet who has followed the cult of Gauguin even as far as Tahiti. Being a handsome man, when he heard the swarthy princess would grant him her favors she showed her joy in the manner in which we have described. Unfortunately, his poems are filled only with their own subjectivities, the Victorian style of the "Georgian Anthology." (my translation)

10. Cf. Lewis's affirmation that "the Vorticist is at his maximum point of energy when stillest" ("Our Vortex" 148).

11. Written in Paris in 1911, the poem was also printed in *Prufrock and Other Observations* (1917) with its current prepositional form, "Rhapsody *on* a Windy Night" (my emphasis).

## Works Cited

Aldington, Richard. "The Poetry of F. S. Flint." *The Egoist* 2 (1 May 1915): 80-81. Print.

Aldington, R., Arbuthnot, L. Atkinson, Gaudier Brzeska, J. Dismorr, G. Hamilton, E. Pound, W. Roberts, H. Sanders, E. Wadsworth, Wyndham Lewis. "Manifesto." *Blast* 1 (1914): 9-43.

Alexander, Michael. *The Poetic Achievement of Ezra Pound*. Berkeley: U of California P, 1979. Print.

Beasley, Rebecca. *Ezra Pound and the Visual Culture of Modernism*. Cambridge: Cambridge UP, 2007. Print.

*Blast: Review of the Great English Vortex* 1 (1914). Ed. Wyndham Lewis. Rpt. in *Blast: Review of the Great English Vortex, Numbers 1-2* (1914-1915). New York: Kraus Reprint Corporation, 1967. Print.

*Blast: Review of the Great English Vortex* 2 (1915). Ed. Wyndham Lewis. Rpt. in *Blast: Review of the Great English Vortex, Numbers 1-2* (1914-1915). New York: Kraus Reprint Corporation, 1967. Print.

Carr, Helen. *The Verse Revolutionaries: Ezra Pound, H.D. and the Imagists*. London: Jonathan Cape, 2009. Print.

Dismorr, Jessie. "London Notes." *Blast* 2 (1915): 66.

---. "Monologue." *Blast* 2 (1915): 65.

Eliot, T. S. *To Criticize the Critic and Other Writings*. London: Faber, 1978. Print.

---. "Preludes." *Blast* 2 (1915): 48-49.

---. "Rhapsody of a Windy Night." *Blast* 2 (1915): 50-51.

Friedman, Susan Stanford. *Psyche Reborn: The Emergence of H.D.*
    Bloomington: Indiana UP, 1987. Print.
Gregory, Eileen. *H.D. and Hellenism, Classic Lines.* New York: Cambridge
    UP, 1997. Print.
Hakutani, Yoshinobu. *Haiku and Modernist Poetics.* New York: Palgrave
    Macmillan, 2009. Print.
H.D. "Oread" [Untitled]. *Blast* 1 (1914): 154.
Hickman, Miranda B. *The Geometry of Modernism: Vorticist Idiom in
    Lewis, Pound, H.D., and Yeats.* Austin: U of Texas P, 2005. Print.
Hueffer, Ford Madox. "The Old Houses of Flanders." *Blast* 2 (1915): 37.
Hughes, Glenn. *Imagism and the Imagists: A Study in Modern Poetry.*
    Stanford UP: Stanford, 1931. Print.
Hulme, T. E. *The Collected Writings of T. E. Hulme.* Ed. Karen Csengeri.
    Oxford: Oxford UP, 1994. Print.
---. "Romanticism and Classicism." *Modernism: A Sourcebook.* Ed. Steven
    Matthews. Houndmills: Palgrave Macmillan, 2008. 157-61. Print.
Kenner, Hugh. *The Pound Era.* Berkeley: U of California P, 1971. Print.
Lewis, Wyndham. "Futurism, Magic and Life." *Blast* 1 (1914): 132-35.
---. "Long Live the Vortex!" *Blast* 1 (1914): 7-8.
---. "Notice to Public." *Blast* 2 (1915): 7.
---. "Our Vortex." *Blast* 1 (1914): 147-49.
Lowell, Amy. Preface. *Some Imagist Poets.* Ed. Lowell. Boston and New
    York: Houghton Mifflin, 1915. v-viii. Print.
Lyotard, Jean-François. *The Differend: Phrases in Dispute.* Trans. Georges
    Van Den Abbeele. Minneapolis: U of Minnesota P, 1988. Print.
Materer, Timothy. "Poetics: Vorticism." *The Ezra Pound Encyclopedia.* Ed.
    Demetres P. Tryphonopoulos and Stephen J. Adams. Westport:
    Greenwood Press, 2005. 231. Print.
McArthur, Murray. "Deciphering Eliot: 'Rhapsody on a Windy Night' and
    the Dialectic of the Cipher." *American Literature* 66.3 (1994): 509-24.
    Print.
Moody, A. David. *The Young Genius, 1885-1920.* Oxford: Oxford UP, 2007.
    Print. Vol. 1 of *Ezra Pound: Poet, A Portrait of the Man & His Work.* 1
    vol. to date.
O'Keefe, Paul. *Some Sort of Genius: A Life of Wyndham Lewis.* London:
    Jonathan Cape, 2000. Print.
Orage, A. R. [R.H.C.]. "Readers and Writers." *The New Age* 15.23 (8 Oct.
    1914): 549-51. Print.
Peppis, Paul. "Schools, Movements, Manifestoes." *The Cambridge
    Companion to Modernist Poetry.* Ed. Alex Davis and Lee M. Jenkins.
    Cambridge: Cambridge UP, 2007. 28-50. Print.
Perloff, Marjorie. *Poetics of Indeterminacy: Rimbaud to Cage.* Princeton:
    Princeton UP, 1981. Print.

Pound, Ezra. "Ancient Music." *Blast* 2 (1915): 20.

---. "Ancient Wisdom, rather cosmic." *Blast* 2 (1915): 22.

---. "Before Sleep." *Blast* 1 (1914): 47.

---. "Dogmatic Statement on the Game and Play of Chess." *Blast* 2 (1915): 19.

---. "Epitaphs." *Blast* 1 (1914): 48.

---. "Et Faim Sallir Le Loup Des Boys." *Blast* 2 (1915): 22.

---. "Fratres Minores." *Blast* 1 (1914): 48.

---. *Gaudier-Brzeska, A Memoir*. New York: New Directions, 1974. Print.

---. *Guide to Kulchur*. New York: New Directions, 1970. Print.

---. "His Vision of a Certain Lady Post Mortem." *Blast* 1 (1914): 48.

---. *Literary Essays of Ezra Pound*. Ed. T. S. Eliot. New York: New Directions, 1968. Print.

---. "Our Contemporaries." *Blast* 2 (1915): 21.

---. "The Seafarer." *Ripostes of Ezra Pound*. London: Ovid Press, 1912. 25-30. Print.

---. *The Selected Letters of Ezra Pound, 1907-1941*. Ed. D. D. Paige. New York: New Directions, 1971. Print.

---. *Selected Prose 1909–1965*. Ed. William Cookson. New York: New Directions, 1973. Print.

---. "Vortex." *Blast* 1 (1914): 153-54.

---. "Vorticism." *Fortnightly Review* ns 573 (1914): 461-71. Print.

Rainey, Lawrence. *The Institutions of Modernism: Literary Elites and Public Culture*. New Haven: Yale UP, 1998. Print.

Stevens, Wallace. "Rubbings of Reality" (1946). *Opus Posthumous*. Ed. Samuel French Morse. Alfred Knopf: New York, 1977. 257-59. Print.

Thacker, Andrew. "'Mad after foreign notions': Ezra Pound, Imagism and the Geography of the Orient." *Geographies of Modernism: Literature, Cultures, Spaces*. Ed. Peter Brooker and Andrew Thacker. London and New York: Routledge, 2005. 31-42. Print.

Wees, William C. "Ezra Pound as a Vorticist." *Wisconsin Studies in Contemporary Literature* 6.1 (1965): 56-72. Print.

Whitworth, Michael H. *Reading Modernist Poetry*. Wiley-Blackwell: Malden, 2010. Print.

# Image, Vortex, Radiant Node:
# Ezra Pound as Lens

Shelley Puhak

The Imagist poets were born during an era of optimistic belief in the power of science and an unprecedented interest in artificial lenses such as the microscope and telescope. They were raised with the means to directly perceive the busy society within a rain puddle, the daily activities of our bodies' cells, and the journeys of celestial bodies. Edmund Dixon, writing in 1857, prophesied, "it seems probable, from many symptoms, that the microscope is about to become the idol of the day; we appear to be on the eve of a microscope mania" (346). And he was correct. The basic design and mechanics of the microscope and telescope changed very little from the sixteenth century until the nineteenth century. However, thanks to advances in optics beginning around 1890, affordable and precise composite microscopes and reflecting telescopes became the norm. Once the property of the "gentleman scientist" of the Victorian era, microscopes and telescopes became increasingly commonplace in middle- and working-class households by the turn of the century. The exploits of amateurs spawned books and newspaper accounts about spinster microscopists, weekend astronomers, and heroic microbe hunters. Families gazed at the stars or squinted at common leaves as a means of self-improvement or even as a way to religious enlightenment.

This new ability to see beyond the confines of the eye is essential to the

Imagists' insistence on accuracy and "direct treatment of the thing." The expansion of human vision alters the directive to render exactly what the eye sees. A telescope that could reveal the outermost stretches of our galaxy and a microscope that could conjure the smallest particles of light and matter changed irrevocably our understanding of the concepts of *accuracy, precision, clarity, scale, degree,* and *focus.*

While every Imagist poet had to be aware of and even inspired by these technological advances, one poet in particular was so struck that he began to see himself as functioning as one of these lenses. Beginning around 1909 and coinciding with his introduction to Hulme, Flint, and the rest of the "Eiffel Tower group," Ezra Pound begins adopting the general rhetoric of science, particularly in his critical prose. In the years leading up to the Imagist declaration and the publication of *Des Imagistes,* Pound shifts from viewing poetry as a science to viewing the poet as a technology in service of science: the artificial lens. Pound's poet-as-lens emerges in his Imagist poems and grows increasingly sophisticated in his Vorticist poems.

## Images Under the Lens

In *The Spirit of Romance,* his first book of prose, published in 1910, Pound makes a tentative statement of the link between poet and scientist: "a number of sciences [are] connected with the study of literature" (vi). That same year, in a review of Hudson Maxim's book *The Science of Poetry and the Philosophy of Language,* he restates this sentiment more emphatically: "poetry *does* admit of scientific analysis and discussion; it *is* subject to law and laws. . . . Poetry admits new and profounder explanations in the light of modern science" (Baechler, Litz, and Longenbach 41).

Pound develops this idea of poetry as a science in the next two years. In his essay "I Gather the Limbs of Osiris," he conflates the two in order to criticize the reigning romantic aesthetic: "science is unpoetic only to minds jaundiced with sentiment and romanticism" (BLL 45). In "Psychology and Troubadours," he begins to see the poet as a scientist, writing, "Hyper-scientific *precision* is the touch-stone and assay of the artist's power and of his honour, of his authenticity" (BLL 84, emphasis mine). In his "Wisdom of Poetry" essay, he distinguishes between the poet and scientist while emphasizing their similar focus. In doing so, he refers to science's newest discoveries: "Our scientist reaching toward a truth speaks of 'the essentials to thought'; these are not poetry, but a constituent substance of poetry . . .

the dynamic particles, *si licet*, this radium" (BLL 73).

Pound's vortexes, cones, and rods are all borrowed from the scientific lingo of the day. References abound in his poetry to biology, botany, astronomy, and medicine. The rhetoric of science underpins so much of his writing that I am hardly the first to examine this link in Pound's work. Various scholars have researched Pound's use of science. Most important is Ian F. A. Bell's book *Critic as Scientist: The Modern Poetics of Ezra Pound*. Although Bell focuses mostly on metaphysics, he does argue that Pound's modernism can be defined by his responses to scientific traditions and discoveries. He also speculates that Pound was motivated to adopt scientific lingo, in part, by his own insecurities; Pound was seeking the respect and adulation bestowed upon scientific pioneers.

More recently, Daniel Albright, in his *Quantum Poetics: Yeats, Pound, Eliot, and the Science of Modernism*, examines how modernist poets used scientific metaphors in their poetry. Daniel Tiffany's book *Radio Corpse: Imagism and the Cryptaesthetic of Ezra Pound* focuses on Pound's early career and interest in the biological sciences. Kimberly Kyle Howey's recent doctoral thesis expands upon some of Tiffany's work. She researches Pound's use of the rhetoric of science and argues that Pound's poetics embraces a modern ideology of science (8).

I am building upon this body of work in examining the influence of a specific scientific technology, the artificial lens, on Pound's work. During the same period of 1909-1912, preceding his involvement with Imagism, Pound also begins focusing on how one should *see*. He declares that the role of the poet is to sharpen and clarify perception for the reader. In 1911, Pound writes in "Osiris": "As for myself, I have tried to clear up a certain messy place in the history of literature; I have tried to make our sentiment of it more *accurate*" (BLL 45, emphasis mine). He goes on to argue in his 1912 "Wisdom of Poetry" that "the function of an art is to strengthen the perceptive faculties and free them from encumbrance" (BLL 73). This insistence upon *accuracy* and *precision* in both observation and description is seen again in his 1914 essay "Vorticism." In this essay, Pound writes of a Russian correspondent who realizes the aims of Imagism after reading the poem "Heather": "I see, you wish to give people new eyes, not to make them see some new particular thing" (BLL 278). These essays all suggest Pound believed his role as poet mimicked that of the artificial lens: both should "unencumber" human vision with "new eyes" that offer enhanced clarity.

Why did Pound make the transition from general scientific rhetoric to the rhetoric of a specific scientific technology? Perhaps he did so simply because it is common for thinkers to describe the workings of their minds in terms of the latest technology. As the journalist Nicholas Carr notes, "When the mechanical clock arrived, people began thinking of their brains as operating 'like clockwork.' Today, in the age of software, we have come to think of them as operating 'like computers.'" At the turn of the century, the Yerkes Observatory opened in Wisconsin with a new 40-inch refractor telescope. Shortly thereafter, in 1903, Zsigmondy created an ultramicroscope that could study objects below the wavelength of light. And just two years before the March 1913 Imagist declaration, the new Ritchey–Chrétien telescope produced detailed photographs of spiral nebulas, still frames of celestial whirling light. So it seems only natural that a writer surrounded by a public that lauded the newest artificial lens, a writer who appreciated his newly-gained access to both the outermost stretches of our galaxy and the smallest particles of light, would begin to see himself as operating as a lens.

We might also consider the way Pound's construction of poet-as-lens was reinforced by his association with H.D. Charlotte Mandel has done wonderful work on the Imagist as "poet-seer," focusing on H.D.'s specific relationship to the lens of the microscope and telescope. H.D.'s grandfather was a microscopist, an expert in micro-botany, and her father, of course, a noted astronomer. Mandel points to the poems "Sea Gods," "Pursuit," "Sea Violet," and "Sea Rose" as examples of how H.D. adopts a scientist's perspective in "naming species," "observing structure," and "demand[ing] that we look closely at small things" (303-04). She persuasively shows how the closing image in "Sea Violet" of a frost-covered violet "uncannily merges the microscope's concentrated magnifying power, the telescope's power to bring a star near at hand, and a cinematic held-shot" (305).

One can see the aesthetic of the lens emerging in H.D.'s earlier work, such as her "Hermes of the Ways" in Des Imagistes, which magnifies grains of sand to show the reader they are indeed "clear as wine" and provides an extreme close-up of the "coarse, salt-crusted grass" (21). Her later Imagist poem "Cities," with its conceit of the beehive, puts under the lens the unseen "seething life" of a honeycomb's cells and asks us to contemplate the smallest particles: "grains of honey, / old dust of stray pollen."

Mandel points out that "the influence of Ezra Pound upon H.D.'s formulation of herself as a poet and as Imagist has generally been assumed as axiom; he could not, however, have been indifferent to her unique style of seeing/phrasing" (310). And it seems significant that of the six poems of his own which Pound included in *Des Imagistes* alongside of H.D.'s work ("Doria," "The Return," "After Ch'u Yuan," "Liu Ch'e," "Fan-Piece for Her Imperial Lord," and "Ts'ai Chi'h") most mimic the microscope and telescope's basic act of magnification. These poems, much like his best-known Imagist poem, "In a Station of the Metro," demonstrate a narrow focus on and enhancement of a single image.

"Liu Ch'e" ostensibly focuses on sound, or rather, the absence of sound, the "the rustling of the silk is discontinued, / . . . there is no sound of foot-fall," and even the leaves that might crackle underfoot have put themselves "into heaps and lie still" (*Personae* 110). Still, Pound uses the visual image to frame the quiet of the scene. He magnifies the courtyard so that we see the "dust [that] drifts" and the "wet leaf that clings to the threshold" (*Personae* 110). In "Fan Piece, For Her Imperial Lord," the "fan of white silk," a metaphor for the speaker and her position as discarded mistress, is compared to something that can only be seen by very close observation: the fan is "clear as frost on the grass-blade" (*Personae* 111).

Perhaps one of the clearest examples of Pound-as-lens from *Des Imagistes* can be found in the three-line modified haiku "Ts'ai Chi'h," which begins with a simple observation: "The petals fall in the fountain" (*Personae* 111). The poet then enlarges this initial image, recasting and reclassifying those petals as "orange-coloured rose-leaves," and then zooms in, noting that "their ochre clings to the stone" (*Personae* 111).

Although not included in *Des Imagistes*, Pound's most famous Imagist poem, "In a Station of the Metro," also focuses on a single image, although rather than enlarging this image, Pound blurs it. In this way, the poem imitates the way a lens focuses on a distant image. While the "faces in the crowd" are first presented in focus, with the merest click (in this case, a line break) the lens loses focus and blurs the image so that it appears to be something else entirely: "petals on a wet, black bough" (*Personae* 111). The design of this poem also borrows from microscopy by bringing something from nature indoors to privilege the act of observing nature out of its usual element: whether people or blossoms, the image is viewed underground.

## A Vortex of "Whirling Light"

The most obvious link between artificial lenses and Pound's ideal of the *Imagiste* poet is that both privilege the visual image. In presenting that image, both poet and lens are necessarily preoccupied with light and its manipulation. In fact, Pound's definition of *phanopoeia*, as he would articulate it years later, is focused on "throwing the object (fixed or moving) onto the visual imagination," much like projecting an image onto a screen (*ABC* 63). If one imagines the "visual imagination" as a projector screen, the act of using *phanopoeia* requires a lens (or a poet-as-lens) to reflect and refract the image onto this screen. The very use of the verb "throw" implies the purposeful use of force, the mastery of light through its manipulation, and it echoes the phrasing of Victorian microscopy manuals. We see this same language in Wood's *Common Objects of the Microscope* when he describes the way the artificial lens perceives an image: "the light is thrown perpendicularly upon the object" (13), and "[it] throw[s] the rays of light straight or obliquely through the object" (22).

Pound's Vorticist poems are a clear extension of this aesthetic. Starting in 1914, Pound-as-critic moves from the metaphor of the static *image* to the more dynamic *vortex*. Similarly, Pound-as-lens moves from simple magnification of the image to images that are wrought from the very act of magnification itself—reflecting, refracting, concentrating, projecting, and "throwing" light onto a plane, whether the plane of specimen slide, page, or imagination. And it is from the perspective of the high-powered lens of the early twentieth century that Pound will create one of his most enduring images, the radiant node.

We most clearly see this shift in poems that focus on movement, often the movement of light itself. Consider two poems from *Blast*, published in 1914 but written during Pound's involvement with Imagism: "Before Sleep" and "The Game of Chess." "Before Sleep" features a speaker caught at the moment of falling asleep, comparing that moment to a descent into the underworld. The poem opens: "The lateral vibrations caress me, / They leap and caress me" (*Personae* 77). Given Pound's practice of adopting scientific rhetoric, it cannot be sheer coincidence that the term "lateral vibrations" was one discussed by some of the most prominent physicists and astronomers of Pound's day. The Chair of Astronomy at Oxford, William Fishburn Donkin, has an entire chapter "On The Lateral Vibrations" in his seminal 1870 work, *Acoustics: Theoretical*, as does John

William Strutt, Cambridge physicist and 1904 Nobel Prize winner, in his 1877 *The Theory of Sound*, a text that is still referred to today. As much as "lateral vibrations" figure into many theories of sound, they were also often discussed by contemporary astronomers trying to craft more powerful and accurate telescopes. One of the earliest of these discussions was begun by Joseph Wharton in his 1865 article in *The American Journal of Science and the Arts*, which postulates that the "lateral vibrations of the *aether*" (191) impacts the way we perceive the light from distant stars. And there is also the constant worry in the literature of the "lateral vibrations" of the glass lens blurring a telescope's field. Given this context, it seems Pound wishes to suggest that the speaker's descent through these "lateral vibrations," though pleasurable, leads to a lack of clarity. The poet-as-lens is anesthetized and compromised by an old and imprecise science.

In the second section of the poem, the speaker ascends, following "light" and "Pallas [Athena]" in his imagination. The goddess's flight is compared to "a rocket," which has the speaker looking skyward, and the rocket's path and its exhaust trail are followed with a telescopic eye: "from right to left and from left to right / in the flat projection of a spiral" (*Personae* 77). The ability of the telescopic lens to focus upon and follow a fast-moving object across a wide-field, without the object being distorted by the "lateral vibrations" of the "aether" or the lens, speaks to recent technological advances in telescopy brought about by the new Ritchey–Chrétien model, invented in 1910. This design is so accurate that it is still in use in the Hubble Space Telescope today.

The poet-as-lens shifts from telescopic to microscopic views in the more muscular "The Game of Chess," which features a chess board "alive with light" (*Personae* 124). The speaker notes the movements of chess pieces from a viewing position somewhere above: "these pieces are living in form, / Their moves break and reform the pattern" (124). The pattern is magnified, not to show a single image, but the movement of light itself: "leaping of bands, straight strips of hard colour, / Blocked light working in" (124). Writing to Harriet Monroe to defend the poem as a Vorticist piece, Pound explained that his aim was "to treat the [chess] pieces as light potentialities" (qtd. in Ruthven 75). The phrasing "light potentialities" and the poem's "bands" and "strips of hard colour" show that Pound was familiar with recent advances in electromagnetic theory, for it was under the high-powered lens that previously unseen wavelengths were broken into "bands" of color.

In the 1918 "Phanopoeia" we also see light portrayed in much the same way, as "wire-like bands of colour" (*Personae* 167). The poet-as-lens perceives light as shimmering "gold" that infuses both water and flame, enveloping the speaker's ascent and descent. Its waves can be broken down to "bands of colour" under the lens. This poem concretely speaks to the transfiguration of light under the lens, and its three sections address the way in which scientific advances changed the way the light is "thrown."

The first section of the poem is titled "Rose White, Yellow, Silver." The poem proceeds to use these colors in a scene describing "the swirl of light": presumably rose-white describes "the smoke of incense," yellow stands for the "gold light" and "gold-coloured flame," and silver is the color of the "ball" that "forms in [his] hand" (167). The speaker states that "The water-jet of gold light bears us up through the ceilings; / Lapped in the gold-coloured flame I descend through the *aether*" (167). Here we again have a speaker descending as in "Before Sleep," but this time explicitly "through the *aether*." It's important to note that *aether* was supposed to be a transmission medium, some undefined substance that filled space, human bodies, and air to allow light, heat, and sound to move from one spot to the next. Maxwell and Hertz, the fathers of electromagnetic theory, believed light waves moved through a specific "luminiferous ether." *Aether* theory was proposed by Aristotle and later championed by Newton; it was the underlying assumption of almost every scientist until it was replaced in the twentieth century by the theory of relativity and quantum theory. So this poem begins with colors as they are perceived by the unaided eye and is rooted in the old science of *aether* theory.

The second section of the poem is titled "Saltus," Latin for "a leap." This title refers to a leap in perception brought about by the artificial lens: "the swirling sphere has opened" (167). The speaker and his companion are no longer enveloped in a flame coursing through *aether*. The "you" has now "perceived the blades of the flame / the flutter of sharp-edged sandals" and has "perceived the leaves of the flame"(167). Once the lens has "opened" up the "swirling sphere," one is able to perceive the components of fire and even catch a glimpse of the divine, signified by Hermes's sandals.

The third section speaks most directly to the idea of the artificial lens; it is titled *concava vallis*, Latin for "concave valley." Every concave lens has a valley at its center, as the edges of the glass are thickest. This "concave valley" is where light rays hit before being reflected outward. This third section opens with the speaker bragging that "The wire-like bands of color involute / mount from my fingers; / I have wrapped the wind round your shoulders" (167). What was merely experienced in the first section, and perceived in the second, is now harnessed: light is broken into its constituent "wire-like bands of color," and the speaker can "wrap the wind" around his beloved as easily as a shawl. The "swirl of light" from the first line of the poem reappears as "the whirling tissue of light," but now it too is navigable: it "grows solid beneath us" (168). The haze of the *aether* in section 1 has been purified into "sea-clear sapphire of air" and "sea-dark *clarity*" (168, emphasis mine).

Pound went beyond the rhetoric and metaphor of the lens in poems such as this to actually "throwing light" with the creation of another artificial lens: the vortoscope. In 1916 he collaborated with the photographer A. L. Coburn to create a photographic machine that produced fractured images out of ordinary materials: wood, glass, or even the human form. They invented this machine by binding together three of Pound's shaving mirrors below a homemade glass light table. The resulting prismatic images were termed "Vortographs," and Coburn and Pound created at least forty of these during the winter of 1916–1917.

Howey argues that "Coburn's initial idea for the invention likely originated from a microscope, and the suffix—'scope' in 'Vortoscope'— further links the camera-device to a technical, machine-like function, as in a scientific microscope" (243). In a 1916 essay, Coburn writes enthusiastically of the function of a microscope: "The beauty of the design displayed by the microscope seems to me a wonderful field to explore from the purely pictorial point of view, the use of prisms for the splitting of images into segments has been very slightly experimented with, and multiple exposures on the same plate . . . have been neglected almost entirely" (qtd. in Howey 243). The aims and the results of the vortoscope that Coburn admires (the split image, fractured light) are remarkably similar to the aims and results of the new higher-powered artificial lenses of the early twentieth century.

## The Radiant Node

Pound's Vorticist poems and his involvement with the vortoscope signal a shift from the basic Victorian lens to the sophisticated lenses of the early twentieth century. Pound-as-lens moves from describing what he observes under the glass, so to speak, to participating in and describing the very mechanisms of that observation. We can also see this shift in the development of Pound's "radiant node." This symbol is rooted in his idea of the scientifically-selected "Luminous Detail" ("Osiris," BLL 44) and later is often interchangeable with his vortex. Perhaps Pound's best-known statement about his "radiant node or cluster" is from his 1914 essay "Vorticism," which links the node back to its Imagist roots: "The image is not an idea. It is a radiant node or cluster; it is what I can, and must perforce, call a VORTEX, from which, and through which, and into which, ideas are constantly rushing" (BLL 283).

The more sophisticated, higher-powered artificial lenses are capable of magnifying not just tangible objects drawn from nature—a leaf, petal, branch—but also the previously invisible components of those objects. The poet-as-lens is able clearly to perceive, and perhaps even to harness, light itself. Consider the process of the ultramicroscope, invented in 1903, to study particles too small to be visible in an ordinary-light microscope. The particles, usually suspended in a liquid, were illuminated with a strong light. The particles scatter this light, and their movements are seen only as flashes against a dark background. The "constituent substance of poetry," Pound wrote of in his "Wisdom of Poetry" essay, the "dynamic particles, *si licet*, this radium" (BLL 73), bears more than just a passing resemblance to these illuminated particles.

Pound began using the radiant node as early as 1908 and continued using it up through the later Cantos. In his uncollected 1908 poem "Plotinus," he writes of "draw[ing] through the node of things / Back sweeping to the vortex of the cone" (qtd. in Ruthven 75). Later, in his uncollected "A Prologue" from 1911, he writes of a "whirling light" (qtd. in Ruthven 192). One can continue to trace this image through his Vorticist poems: the "whirl[ing]" chess pieces in "The Game of Chess," including a "King down in the vortex" (*Personae* 124); the "whirling laughter" in "Provincia Deserta" (*Personae* 125); and the "swirl of light," "swirling sphere," and "whirling tissue of light" in "Phanopoeia" (*Personae* 167-68). In all of these instances, Pound's radiant node is a dynamic image, constantly in flux and produced by the rapid exchange of energy. Like the lens of the ultra-microscope, the radiant node creates an abstraction out of light at the very moment it brings order to it. And, as many have noted, this tension lies at the heart of so much of Pound's work.

Much later, in his 1928 essay "Cavalcanti," he writes of the node: "We appear to have lost the radiant world where one thought cuts through another with a clean edge, a world of moving energies . . . magnetisms that take form, that are seen, or that border the visible" (154). This later phrasing most clearly aligns the node with its astronomical roots: the intersection of an orbit with a plane. This meaning dates back to the 1660s, but by the time Pound wrote of his radiant cluster, "node" was being used to indicate various intersections of forces and objects in the fields of physics, botany, anatomy, and mathematics. So the node also serves as an apt metaphor for Pound's much desired intersection of poetry and science.

The "radiant node" will continue to appear through Pound's work all the way up until his late Cantos. Canto 91 speaks of "the light flowing, whelming the stars" (633). And K. K. Ruthven notes that Canto 93 returns to an image from the 1918 "Phanopoeia": "the light there almost solid," echoing "the whirling tissue of light" that now "grows solid beneath us" (192). Canto 106 describes light as a swelling seed, a "great acorn of light bulging outward" (775), and Canto 116 asks, "Can you enter the great acorn of light?" (815). This image of a seed is yet another transfiguration of light from a perspective that is dependent upon *accuracy, precision,* and *clarity* and that requires the poet to manipulate *scale, degree,* and *focus*. It is important to note that Pound was writing this many years after spiral structures of newly photographed nebula appeared in newspapers, and shortly after Hubble's discovery of galaxies other than our own. "The great acorn of light" is quite a literal reference, if one considers how these newly discovered worlds appeared through the artificial lens. Galaxies viewed through the lens have three parts: a disk of seemingly solid light, a halo, and a "bulging" nucleus. Pound's radiant node, initially perceived as blurred light or a splotch of moving energy, gradually becomes "solid," much like the spiral arms of a galaxy. Eventually, as the lens becomes capable of even greater clarity, it reveals what lies in the center: a nucleus that is, truly, an "acorn of light bulging."

As a young poet, Pound had declared, "Light! / I am up to follow thee, Pallas" (*Personae* 77). Throughout his work he seems to pursue the very same thing as the microbe hunters and spinster astronomers of his youth. His hyper-focus on the image, the vortex, and the radiant node is an attempt to recreate a "radiant world . . . a world of moving energies" ("Cavalcanti" 154) and to explore the life force that lies at its center. Pound's aims perfectly align with those of the artificial lenses of the early twentieth century: to capture, in the words of the bestselling *Common Objects of the Microscope*, "the soft, glowing radiance, the delicate pearly translucence, or the flashing effulgence of living and ever-changing light" (Wood iv).

## Works Cited

Albright, Daniel. *Quantum Poetics: Yeats, Pound, Eliot, and the Science of Modernism.* Cambridge UP, 1997. Print.

Baechler, Lea, A. Walton Litz, and James Longenbach, eds. *Ezra Pound's Poetry and Prose Contributions to Periodicals.* Vol 1. New York: Garland, 1991. Print.

Bell, Ian F. A. *Critic as Scientist: The Modernist Poetics of Ezra Pound.* London: Metheun, 1981. Print.

Carr, Nicholas. "Is Google Making Us Stupid?" *The Atlantic Monthly* (July/ August 2008). Web. 2 May 2010.

Dixon, Edmund Saul. "Microscopic Preparations." *Household Words* 16 (1857). Rpt. in The Living Age 55 (1858): 346-52. Web. 10 October 2011.

Donkin, William Fishburn. *Acoustics: Theoretical.* Oxford UP: 1870. Web. 23 May 2010.

H.D. "Cities." *Poetry Foundation.Org.* Web. 11 October 2011.

---. "Hermes of the Ways." *Des Imagistes.* New York: Albert and Charles Boni, 1914. 21-23. Web. 10 May 2010.

Howey, Kimberly Kyle. *Ezra Pound and the Rhetoric of Science, 1901–1922.* Diss. University College London, 2009. Print.

Mandel, Charlotte. "Magical Lens: Poet's vision beyond the naked eye." *H.D. Woman and Poet.* Ed. Michael King. Orono, ME.: National Poetry Foundation, 1986: 301-17. Print.

Pound, Ezra. *ABC of Reading.* New York: New Directions, 1987. Print.

---. *The Cantos of Ezra Pound.* New York: New Directions, 1995. Print.

---. "Cavalcanti." *The Dial* (1928): 24. Rpt. in *Literary Essays of Ezra Pound.* 1954. Ed. T. S. Eliot. New York: New Directions, 1972. 154. Print.

---. "I Gather the Limbs of Osiris." *The New Age* 10 (1911-1912): 107, 130-31, 155-56, 178-80, 201-02, 224-25, 249-51, 274-75, 297-99, 343-44, 369-70, 392-93. Rpt. in Baechler, Litz, and Longenbach 43-58, 67-71.

---. *Personae: The Shorter Poems of Ezra Pound.* Rev. ed. Ed. Lea Baechler and A. Walton Litz. New York: New Directions, 1990. Print.

---. "Psychology and Troubadours." *Quest* 4.1 (1912): 37–53. Rpt. in Baechler, Litz, and Longenbach 83-99.

---. "The Science of Poetry." *Book News Monthly* 29.4 (1910): 282-83. Rpt. in Baechler, Litz, and Longenbach 40-41.

---. *The Spirit of Romance: An Attempt to Define Somewhat the Charm of* the *Pre-Renaissance Literature of Latin Europe*. London: J. M. Dent & Sons, 1910. Print.

---. "Vorticism." *Fortnightly Review* ns. 96 (1914): 461-71. Rpt. in Baechler, Litz, and Longenbach 275-85.

---. "The Wisdom of Poetry." *Forum* 47.4 (1912): 497–501. Rpt. in Baechler, Litz, and Longenbach 72–75.

Ruthven, K. K. *A Guide to Ezra Pound's* Personae. Berkeley: U of California P, 1969. Print.

Strutt, John William. *The Theory of Sound*. 2 vol. Cambridge UP, 1877. Web. 23 May 2010.

Tiffany, Daniel. *Radio Corpse: Imagism and the Cryptaesthetic of Ezra Pound*. Harvard UP, 1995. Print.

Wharton, Joseph. "Speculations upon a possible method of determining the distance of certain variably colored stars." *The American Journal of Science and the Arts* 40.1 (1865): 191. Web. 10 October 2011.

Wood, Rev. J. G. *Common Objects of the Microscope*. London: George Routledge and Sons, 1861. Archive.Org. Web. 15 May 2010.

# II. Imagism: Impact

# "Poetry Which Moves By Its Music": Keeping Time with Pound's Imagism

Alex Shakespeare

Ezra Pound's affinity for music is well documented. An incomplete catalogue of his musical interests would note his enduring passion for the Provençal troubadours, his vocal support of Arnold Dolmetsch's revival of seventeenth-century music and Olga Rudge's revival of Antonio Vivaldi, and his various operas, musical pieces, and book on the musical avant-garde, *Antheil and the Treatise on Harmony* (1924). Perhaps most significant to the years surrounding Imagism and *Des Imagistes*, however, is his involvement with W. B. Yeats.

Of course, Yeats was already an inspiration to Pound when the two of them met in 1909. But from the moment Pound arrived in London the year before, he had anticipated meeting the author of *The Wind Among the Reeds*, the Yeats whose romantic idiom Pound had been imitating in his own early verse, but instead he met an elder poet who was transforming himself from a Romantic to a modern: a man "in transit I think from the '*dolce stile*' to the '*stile grande*,'" as Pound wrote in November 1910 (Longenbach 17). From 1909 on, Yeats was becoming less interested in his personal experience as a poet of the nineties and more interested in the history and myths surrounding the ancient English and Celtic bards. As a twenty-five-year-old who had recently taken a walking tour of southern France along the same roads walked by the troubadours, Pound was enthusiastic about Yeats's desire to return poetry to "the people" and his movement away from the 1890s art-for-art's-sake aesthetics, which Pound himself had once embraced. In his management of the Abbey Theatre in Dublin and his experiments with chanting and music-accompanied performances in London, Yeats was in the years Pound first knew him eager to renew "a bardic compact to return the poetic voice to the center of culture—on its platforms, stages, and street corners, in a poetry and drama that speak to all classes of the reading and non-reading citizenry" (Schuchard xxi). And Yeats's idea of poetry as a center of culture, a music belonging on every street corner and stage, confirmed Pound's convictions that poetry could have a social purpose, that the poet could sing and be heard.

Not that Pound himself could sing. But he could *talk*. In 1909 especially, he made a deep impression on Yeats's London circle by giving impromptu lectures on prosody and music. At Yeats's Monday Evening gatherings, the poet Douglas Golding recalled Ezra's domination of the room, how he "laid down the law about poetry." When Thomas Sturge Moore (a poet forty years Pound's elder) attempted to speak about prosody, "Ezra reduced him to a glum silence" (Schuchard 264). Yeats himself wrote to Lady Gregory, his lifelong confidante, of "that queer creature Ezra Pound, who has become really a great authority on the troubadours, has I think got closer to the right sort of music for poetry . . . it is definitely music with strongly marked time & yet it is effective speech." Yeats added: "However he can't sing as he has no voice. It is like something on a very bad phonograph" (264).

Even as Pound made his impression on Yeats and his circle, they made their respective impressions on him. Rabindrath Tagore, Bengali poet-musician and London literary sensation, became an intimate of the Yeats circle in 1913 (also the year Tagore won the Nobel Prize), when Pound was able to meet and talk with him about his songs. He even had Tagore "sing and explain to him [in their original Bengali]" (Moody 200). The man interested him, Pound's biographer writes, as "a seeker after 'fundamental laws in word music' [Pound's words] and seemed to correspond to the sort of metric he was working for in English" (200). Pound had a similarly keen interest in the work of actress Florence Farr (longtime musical collaborator with Yeats) and the musical instruments and musical experiments of Arnold Dolmetsch.[1] But most of all, it seems his interest was in Yeats's bardic mystique, his utter commitment to poetry as a way of singing to the "hoi polloi." As James Longebach chronicles in *Stone Cottage*, the "secret society" formed by Pound and Yeats during their winters at Stone Cottage, Sussex was for Pound the most memorable experience of these years (257). Between 1913 and 1916, Pound read aloud to Yeats (from works as varied as Wordsworth, *Dracula*, and *Travels in Arabia Deserta*), revised Yeats's poems and wrote plays intended to be performed alongside Yeats's, and conspired with Yeats to bring poetry back into the realm of public art while bringing the undeniable force of song back into poetry, as Yeats expressed in his last letter: "You can refute Hegel, but not the Saint or the Song of Sixpence" (Wade 922).

Pound was not so much concerned with a technical renovation of poetry *as* music, or with merely emphasizing the musical elements of poetry. He was concerned with developing a new idea of poetry altogether. Certainly the term "Imagism" (and to some degree, "Vorticism") suggests to many readers that Pound's primary concern was with poetry as a collection of images—the art of juxtaposition Hugh Kenner finds illustrated in the two lines of Pound's "In a Station of the Metro." Indeed, in describing the aims of his new poetics, he used the metaphor of sculpture at least as often as music. But the two metaphors should not be confused and thus dismissed as equivocation. For Pound insisted precisely that a poem's music, or *melopoeia*, was a technical element separable from its imagery (*phanopoeia*) and/or its wordplay (*logopoeia*)—a technical triumvirate first proposed in the essay "In the Vortex," where he defined *melopoeia* as "poetry which moves by its music, whether it be a music in the words or an aptitude for, or suggestion of, accompanying music" (*Instigations* 234).[2] For Pound, a poem's "meter" (which he considered an inferior term) was inseparable from a poem's "rhythm" or "music." Thus in the third principle of Imagism, written several years before "In the Vortex," Pound does not refer to prosody in an academic sense but in a vaguely "musical" one: "As regarding rhythm, to compose in the sequence of the musical phrase, not in sequence of a metronome" (*Early Writings* 210).

Imagism was not merely fodder for Pound's manifestoes, but was a "principle" manifest in the works of all the ages and within the worldwide tradition of writing poetry. In a review of Yeats's *Responsibilities* in 1914, for instance, Pound praises the *imagiste* "quality of hard light" in the beginning of Yeats's "The Magi":

Now as at all times I can see in the mind's eye,

In their stiff, painted clothes, the pale unsatisfied ones
Appear and disappear in the blue depth of the sky
With all their ancient faces like rain-beaten stones,
And all their helms of silver hovering side by side. [WBY]

Of course a passage like that, a passage of *imagisme*, may occur
in a poem not otherwise *imagiste*, in the same way that a lyrical
passage may occur in a narrative, or in some poem not otherwise
lyrical. There have always been two sorts of poetry which are, for
me at least, the most "poetic"; they are firstly, the sort of poetry
which seems to be music just forcing itself into articulate speech,
and, secondly, that sort of poetry which seems as if sculpture or
painting were just forced or forcing itself into words. (*Literary
Essays* 380)

The competing metaphors of sculpture and music here—each of them
"just forced into words"—exemplify Pound's dual conception of poetry as
it developed in the 1910s, during and after his closest friendship with Yeats.
Later, sculpture became his concept of *phanopoeia*, music his concept of
*melopoeia*. (*Logopoiea* seems not concretely to have been formulated
until "In the Vortex.") Terminology aside, the point for Pound was that
Yeats's "Magi" seemed to "appear and disappear," like ancient sculpture and
ancient music "just forced or forcing itself into words."

By 1912, Pound began to shun Yeats's romantic imagery—sailors,
horsemen, unhappy lovers, "all of them a multitude out of other days"—
and to incorporate more modern subjects (Schuchard 331). Some of the
most enduring of Pound's 1910s poetry speaks, or sings, in counterpoint,
sounding alternately ancient and modern. The two tones are counterpoised
in the most famous Imagist poem, "In a Station of the Metro," where the
modernism of the title descends to the haiku-like natural simplicity of the
second line:

The apparition of these faces in the crowd:
Petals on a wet, black bough.

The poem is miniscule in the manner of Dutch miniatures; its mastery
is, as witnessed by the seemingly endless possibility of apt interpretations,

precisely its well-wrought details. "This tiny poem," as Hugh Kenner describes it,

> drawing on Gauguin and on Japan, on ghosts and on Persephone, on the Underworld and on the Underground, the metro of Mallarmé's capital and a phrase that names a station of the Metro as it might a station of the Cross, concentrates far more than it need ever specify, and indicates the means of delivering post-Symbolist poetry from its pictorialist impasse. (*The Pound Era* 185)

But the means of delivering the post-Symbolist pictorialist impasse into *what*? Into a musical modernism would be too convenient an answer. I would say instead that Pound delivered—via Imagism, and then Vorticism—his own post-Symbolism (as Kenner calls it) from a late-nineteenth-century fascination with pictorial stasis into a twentieth-century *kinema*: a partly sculpted, partly musical translation of the ancient into a modernist idiom. But the question remains how Pound's ideas about tone, rhythm, and harmony—most of which seem concerned with the troubadours, with seventeenth-century music, and with ancient bards—intersect with his ideas about literary modernism.

In his book on Pound and music, the composer R. Murray Schafer praises Pound's *Treatise on Harmony* as one of the three significant "contributions to the science of harmony in our century" (293) and places Pound in the avant-garde company of Schoenberg, Schenker, Rameau, and Janácek.[3] Schafer adds that, since the writings of these composer/theorists were practically unknown, Pound "may almost certainly be credited with coming on his conceptions simply by the grace of his own good ears" (294). And absolutely central to Schafer's high praise for Pound's "good ears" is Pound's attention to the musical element of *time* and *timing*. Pound's *Treatise* begins: "The element most grossly omitted from treatises on harmony up to the present time is the element of TIME" (qtd. in Schafer 294). The ancient musicians, Pound continues, "thought of music as travelling rhythm going through points or barriers of pitch and pitch-combinations" (qtd. in Schafer 297). That is, ancient musicians thought of music as a forward motion in space as well as time—a fitting companion to Pound's own dual metaphors of sculpture and music.

Holding both metaphors together, however, is Pound's concern with the element of TIME, with the return of ancient things. "It is quite obvious that we do not all of us inhabit the same time," Pound wrote (*Literary Essays* 87). Thus the ancient musicians, the medieval troubadours of Provence, could represent to Pound the (relatively timeless) precursors to his modernism. They could be as much modernists as he, just as Yeats could be an unintentional Imagist. In the notebooks he kept on his 1912 walking tour through southern France, Pound mused:

> Perhaps we exist as the notes of the string exist for a [E natural (Pound draws the note on the treble clef)] is always an [E natural] whoever or whatever strikes it. And tho' it is in a sense the same it is different on different instruments & perhaps our sequence of lives has this in common with the music that we [are] struck upon divers times & give sounds of diverse timbre in response to the striking. (Sieburth 68)

A similar sense of the eternal oneness inherent in human expression rules over time travel in *The Cantos*. One might even venture to say that Pound's notion that "tho' it is in a sense the same it is different on different instruments & perhaps our sequence of lives has this in common with the music . . . [of] divers times" is a key to understanding his modernism as a dynamic verb, instead of a stultified "–ism": not modernism as historical period, but modernism as an active force of the imagination.

In the making of a poem, a musical "sequence" of *lines* therefore provided the means of contact with the *lives* of ancients at the same time that it provided the means of distinguishing oneself from the ancients, as a modern. Unlike Yeats, Pound could imagine the revival of bardic arts—or at least the revival of poetry as a kind of song—as a means to modernism rather than as a purely antiquarian pleasure. The point, for Pound, was to make the troubadours new rather than to make his own poetry *seem* old. Imitations of ancient harmonies, rhythms, and meters could be incorporated into the modernist movement, or the particular "mouvemong" (as Richard Aldington called it) of Imagism. Probably the most apparent means of making a modern poem, in Pound's sense of it, is through indirect translation from an older text or texts—an adaptation of antiquated music to modern purpose.

Contained in the work of translation is an elaborate engagement with the sense of literary "tradition" Eliot formulated in "Tradition and the Individual Talent" (1919)—what Pound seven years earlier had called "the traditional methods." *Tradition*, at its root, connotes a hand-me-down, yet, as Geoffrey Hill puts it: "When Pound writes 'traditional methods' he does not mean 'derivative convention.' In 1912, no less than at the present day, this was a distinction not easily impressed upon the consensus" (248). Then one could say that Pound's modernism is not *institutionally* but *radically* traditional. "To break the pentameter, that was the first heave" sounds deceptively aggravated with the past. What Pound primarily intended to "break" was the Swinburne-rapt music of his own "In Morte De," published in *A Lume Spento* (1908):

Oh wine-sweet ghost how are we borne apart
Of winds that restless blow we know not where
As little shadows smoke-wraith-sudden start
If music break the freighted dream of air. (*Early Writings* 29)

In 1912, Pound was out to break the freighted dream of iambs—not least of all his own—with the manifestoes and the manifest work of Imagism.

Perhaps the most apposite of Pound's imagist poems to compare with Yeats's "The Magi" (which Pound considered such a marvelous, albeit accidental, example of Imagism) is "The Return." One of the original poems of *Des Imagistes*, its confluence of Sapphic classicism—Yeats himself wrote that the poem sounded as if Pound were "translating at sight from an unknown Greek masterpiece" ("Introduction" 193)—and modernist free verse connects ancient music to early twentieth-century experimentation:

The Return

See, they return; ah, see the tentative
Movements, and the slow feet,
The trouble in the pace and the uncertain
Wavering!

See, they return, one, and by one,
With fear, as half-awakened;

As if the snow should hesitate
And murmur in the wind,
             and half turn back;
These were the "Wing'd-with-Awe,"
             Inviolable.

Gods of the winged shoe!
With them the silver hounds,
             sniffing the trace of air!

Haie! Haie!
             These were the swift to harry;
These the keen-scented;
These were the souls of blood.

Slow on the leash,
             pallid the leash-men!
                        (*Des Imagistes* 42)

Kenner writes of the poem that "every line has a strongly marked expressive rhythm but no two lines are alike"; "it is actually the rhythm that defines the meaning" (*The Pound Era* 189). One extrapolates that some of the *sources* of those rhythms, too, form and inform how rhythm defines meaning.

One might hear an echo of Sir Thomas Wyatt's "They flee from me that sometime did me seek / With naked foot, stalking in my chamber" (73) or the enraptured music of Swinburne's "Saphhics." But Swinburne's poem renders exactly the *meter* of the Sapphic hendecasyllabic stanza in English. For instance:

Saw the white implacable Aphrodite,
Saw the hair unbound and the feet unsandalled
Shine as fire of sunset on western waters;
             Saw the reluctant

Feet, the straining plumes of the doves that drew her. (488)

And so on. ("Feet" are virtually an obsession in this poem; later, he has "flying feet," "awful / Sound of feet.") And Swinburne's enjambment—"Saw the reluctant / Feet"— finds itself "translated" into Pound's:

> ah, see the tentative
> Movements, and the slow feet,
> The trouble in the pace and the uncertain
> Wavering!

Caught up in the Sapphic rhythm, Swinburne was not necessarily considering foremost the dramatic power of his "reluctant / Feet." But Pound seizes upon it, and—always the educator—doubles the enjambment to make sure we know the placement is intentional: "tentative / Movements," "uncertain / Wavering."

Kenner hypothesizes that "The Return" (as it is arranged on the page, for the eye) imitates a torn Papyrus, but musically, too, it imitates Greek hendecasyllabic verse—musically but not metrically. In Pound's free verse, as Kenner writes in *The Poetry of Ezra Pound*, "the structural unit" is "the single line (each line, that is to say . . . calls fairly dramatic attention to its point of ending)" (154). So each line processes a discrete thought:

> See, they return, one, and by one,
> With fear, as half-awakened;
> As if the snow should hesitate
> And murmur in the wind,
>                and half turn back[.]

"With fear" modifies the stark act of "return" described in the line above it. "As if the snow should hesitate" modifies the image of "the return" yet again (the ones returning suddenly rendered more ghostly white by the image of snow). And the line itself hesitates at its end. Finally, the fragmentary indented line "and half turn back;" gives us the *sostenuto* of a semicolon, another hesitation of the returning figures.

When toward the end of the poem the rhythm turns from hesitation to exclamation, rhetorical figures as befit the grandeur of resurrection (the anaphora of "These were . . . These . . . These were," the epistrophe of the last lines) are musically accented and pronounced. The pastness of the gods that *were* seems neatly undone by the sure finality of the last two lines. The return has been accomplished not only in the language but in the rhythm of the poem itself, so that "The Return" not only describes a vision of the past (as Yeats does in "The Magi") but dramatizes it, modernizes it, line by line.

In its careful variation of line-length and indentation, Pound's poem moves by its music. Though fixated by the past's return—fixated, in a sense, on keeping time—the poem also effectively anticipates Pound's future in *The Cantos*, whose music is composed by the indentation of lines, the integrated music of foreign tongues, and a complete revolution of how a poem sings:

> Small birds sing in chorus,
> Harmony is in the proportion of branches
>             as clarity (chao¹).⁴ (*The Cantos* 728)

Yet whether we should finally compare Pound's free verse to ancient musical notations, as if it indicated the placement of varying scales or tones, or, on the other hand, compare it to sculpture, as does Donald Davie, seems a question worth asking, though not worth answering. After all, if Pound did not trouble himself to choose either the visual or the musical as modernist poetry's sister art, I see no reason why readers should have to make the choice on his behalf. Still, by *listening* to Pound's Imagist poems (not only reading, analyzing, interpreting, source-hunting), one may hear the music of the twentieth century having "just forced, or forcing itself into words."

## Notes

1. Pound's support of Dolmetsch extended to financial support, even when the poet was young and money was especially scarce. When Pound and Dorothy Shakespear married in April 1914, Yeats gave the couple a sum of money. With it, Pound purchased a clavichord from Arnold Dolmetsch: "we hope it will flower into deathless music," he wrote Yeats; then he slipped from music to image again, "or at least into an image of more gracious and stately times" (Longenbach 100).

2. This was not merely a young artist's passing fancy for formal definitions of poetry. Pound remained interested in poetry's musicality all his life. In his 1962 *Paris Review* interview with Pound, Donald Hall pressed him on the separation of form and content. "I think I've covered that," Pound answered: "[Technique, or form] must be regarded as exercise. Richter in his *Treatise on Harmony*, you see, says 'These are the principles of harmony and

counterpoint; they have nothing whatever to do with composition, which is quite a separate activity'" (Gourevitch 53).

3. Of course, not everyone considered Pound's musical affinities to be serious, at least not in the way that his poetry was serious. Ernest Hemingway in his "Homage to Ezra" called Pound "among other things, a composer [who] has done a splendid opera on Villon." "But I feel about Pound and music something like about M. Constantin Brancusi and cooking," Hemingway continued. "M. Brancusi is a famous sculptor who is also a very famous cook. Cooking is, of course, an art. But it would be lamentable if M. Brancusi would give up sculpture for it or even devote the major part of his time to cookery" (Bruccoli and Baughman 6).

4. Kenner originates the theory that the poems of *Des Imagistes*, *Cathay*, and later the *Homage to Sextus Propertius* form for Pound an increasing prosodic mastery that leads to the mature work of *The Cantos*. In any case, the experiments with line endings, line placement, and defamiliarized metrics point to the distinctly Poundian imprint on Modernism at large. These poems point the way in which T. S. Eliot's *Waste Land*, for instance, must be read as musically, though perhaps not substantially, Ezra Pound's poetry. One need only note and listen to the line breaks of "Prufrock" or "Ash Wednesday" to see their less jagged, and to some degree less Poundian, edge.

## Works Cited

Bruccoli, Matthew, and Judith Baughman, eds. *Hemingway and the Mechanism of Fame*. Columbia, SC: U of South Carolina P, 2006. Print.
Gourevitch, Peter. *The Paris Review Interviews IV*. New York: Picador, 2009. Print.
Hill, Geoffrey. *Collected Critical Writings*. New York: Oxford UP, 2008. Print.
Kenner, Hugh. *The Poetry of Ezra Pound*. U of Nebraska P, 1985. Print.
---. *The Pound Era*. Berkeley: U of California P, 1971. Print.
Longenbach, James. *Stone Cottage*. New York: Oxford UP, 1988. Print.
Moody, A. David. *The Young Genius, 1885-1920*. Oxford: Oxford UP, 2007. Print. Vol. 1 of *Ezra Pound: Poet, A Portrait of the Man & His Work*. 1 vol. to date.
Pound, Ezra. *The Cantos of Ezra Pound*. New York: New Directions, 1972. Print.
---, ed. *Des Imagistes: An Anthology*. New York: Albert and Charles Boni, 1914. Print.
---. *Early Writings*. New York: Penguin, 2005. Print.
---. *Instigations*. New York: Boni and Liveright, 1920. Print.
---. *Literary Essays*. New York: New Directions, 1935. Print.
---. *Personae: The Shorter Poems of Ezra Pound*. Rev. ed. Ed. Lea Baechler

and A. Walton Litz. New York: New Directions, 1990. Print.

Schafer, R. Murray. *Ezra Pound and Music*. New York: New Directions, 1977. Print.

Schuchard, Ronald. *The Last Minstrels: Yeats and the Revival of the Bardic Arts*. New York: Oxford UP, 2008. Print.

Sieburth, Richard. *A Walking Tour in Southern France*. New York: New Directions, 1992. Print.

Swinburne, C. Algernon. *Selections from the Poetical Works*. Ed. R. H. Stoddard. New York: Thomas Y. Crowell, 1884. Print.

Wade, Allen, ed. *The Letters of W. B. Yeats*. New York: Macmillan, 1955. Print.

Wyatt, Thomas. *The Complete Poems*. New York: Penguin, 1995. Print.

Yeats, W. B. "Introduction to The Oxford Book of Modern Verse." *Later Essays: The Collected Works of W. B. Yeats*. Ed. William H. O'Donnell. Vol. 5. New York: Scribner, 1994. 181-203. Print.

# Imagism vs. Impressionism:
# Ezra Pound and Ford Madox Ford

Max Saunders

Ford Madox Ford—or "Hueffer", as he was until 1919—was closely associated with the Imagists and with Imagism. The 1914 anthology *Des Imagistes* included two of his poems. Aldington's *Imagist Anthology* of 1930 included another two, as well as a preface by Ford reminiscing about the movement. His thirty-year friendship with Pound is well-documented, especially in the volume *Pound/Ford*. And though he saw less of Aldington, and seems to have lost touch with H.D. after the war, in the early days of Imagism they were all very close. Both H.D. and Aldington acted as amanuenses when Ford was dictating one of his best novels, *The Good Soldier*. She appears to have collapsed from the strain, so Aldington took over; and he continued to act as Ford's secretary when he was writing propaganda during the first year of the war.[1]

Yet Ford was an improbable Imagist. Aldington said of his pre-war work: "we liked his poems, though there was nothing very imagistic about them until he started to imitate H.D." (*Life for Life's Sake* 124). Indeed Ford's relationship to both Aldington and Pound was conducted through a form of poetic repartee. One of his poems in the volume *Des Imagistes* was an anonymous satire addressed to Aldington, responding to Aldington's inclusion in the same volume of his satire of what is perhaps Ford's best-known poem, "On Heaven"—a poem which, for all its virtues, is too long and conversational for Imagism.[2] The turning point, literally, in Ford's relationship with Pound appears to have come when Pound came to visit Ford in Giessen in August 1911 and showed him his latest volume of verse—probably *Canzoni*—which caused Ford to roll about on the floor. Whether in agony or hilarity isn't clear, but if Pound was mortified, he was also massively grateful, saying that these early poems

> displayed me trapped, fly-papered, gummed and strapped down in a jejune provincial effort to learn, *mehercule*, the stilted language that then passed for "good English" in the arthritic milieu that held control of the respected British critical circles. . .
>
> And that roll saved me at least two years, perhaps more. It sent me back to my own proper effort, namely, toward using the living tongue (with younger men after me), though none of us has found a more natural language than Ford did.[3] (*Selected Prose* 462)

On the other hand, as we shall see, Pound could also object to Ford's language as too natural, playfully criticizing it (in a way akin to Aldington's parody), as when, two years later, in an aesthetic edict headed "A Few Don'ts," he wrote, "Don't use such an expression as 'dim lands of peace.' It dulls the image" ("A Retrospect" 5)—though without identifying the phrase as from a poem of Ford's, "On a Marsh Road," from 1904 (*Selected Poems* 35).

Ford was certainly a champion of Imagism. He wrote two admiring notices of the other poets in the *Des Imagistes* volume, which show him as one of the first to understand the significance of Imagism and as a pioneer in the theorizing of modernist poetics (*Critical Essays* 150-58). But his relation to Imagism is best understood in terms of a productive conflict between the ideas of Imagism and the Impressionism with which Ford came to identify himself.

Literary Impressionism has become newly interesting to recent critics, and there are fine books on its prose fiction by Paul Armstrong, Jesse Matz, and Tamar Katz among others.[4] But Ford was a more explicit and prolific expounder of Impressionism than any of the other authors discussed in these studies, and the significance of his contribution is only beginning to be recognized. The importance of Fordian Impressionism in the development of Pound's poetry, from Imagism on, and the effect of Pound's criticisms on Ford's refining of Impressionism are the reciprocal stories this essay concentrates upon.

Pound wrote two appreciative reviews of Ford's 1913 *Collected Poems*, saying in the first that "we would not be far wrong in calling Mr. Hueffer the best lyrist in England" (*Pound/Ford* 15), and in the second calling him "the best critic in England, one might say the only critic of any importance" (*Pound/Ford* 16). He had even got comically shirty earlier in 1913 when Alice Corbin Henderson had compared Ford with Aldington, telling her,

> Fer Gorrds sake don't compare the infant Richard, dilectus fillius etc. in the year one of his age to F.M.H. an artist mature, accomplished. perhaps [*sic*] the most accomplished writer in England. Almost a Great man, one is constantly trying to find why one can not apply just that word to the most intelligent of ones friends. (*Letters of Ezra Pound to Alice Corbin Henderson* 52)

Yet in March the previous year Pound had already distanced himself from Ford's method, arguing,

> His flaw is the flaw of impressionism, impressionism, that is, carried out of its due medium. Impressionism belongs in paint, it is of the eye. The cinematograph records, for instance, the "impression" of any given action or place, far more exactly than the finest writing, it transmits the impression to its "audience" with less work on their part. A ball of gold and a gilded ball give the same "impression" to the painter. Poetry is in some odd way concerned with the specific gravity of things, with their nature. (*Pound/Ford* 10)

Ten years later, after the war and after *Hugh Selwyn Mauberley*, Pound was taking stock of his debts to Ford in much the same terms.[5] Ford's criticism is decisive, especially for its commitment to a poetic language that was "at least speakable." But his Impressionism is still seen as undermining these strengths: "I think Hueffer goes wrong because he bases his criticism on the eye, and almost solely on the eye," says Pound in 1923 ("On Criticism in General," qtd. in *Pound/Ford* 68).

There are four main thrusts to Pound's critique: Impressionism is too visual, too superficial, too relaxed and discursive, and too passive. It's true that Ford's poetry of this period is markedly conversational, low-key. Take the throwaway opening of "The Starling" from the 1912 collection *High Germany* that Pound had been reviewing:

> It's an odd thing how one changes! . . .
> Walking along the upper ranges
> Of this land of plains
> In this month of rains,
> On a drying road where the poplars march along,
> Suddenly,
> With a rush of wings flew down a company,
> A multitude, throng upon throng,
> Of starlings,
> Successive orchestras of wind-blown song,
> Whirled, like a babble of surf,
> On to the roadside turf—[.]
>                     (*Selected Poems* 55)

Yet if there's a strong visual element there—in the images of the marching poplars, or the surf, say—they're, neither of them, purely visual images. Poplars, after all, don't march: here they are the markers against which human movement is measured. And the "babble of surf" is an image for the noise of the rush of wings and warbles in the wind.

Pound's criticisms of Ford might then seem to apply better to his fiction. *The Good Soldier* is certainly preoccupied with visual surfaces rendered with Impressionistic obliqueness. The narrator, John Dowell, is certainly passive and ineffectual, and for years he lives deceived by the superficial glamour of the "good people" of his set. And his narration is certainly relaxed and conversational, to the point of rambling and contradicting itself. However, Impressionism takes many forms. According to Richard Bretell, there are two main modes of it in painting: what he calls transparent and mediated Impressionism (*Modern Art* 17-18). The transparent version is more concerned with the visual field and takes its visual sensations indiscriminately from the natural world, rivers, trees, haystacks, flowers, or people, as typified by Monet. Mediated Impressionism is much more concerned with social spaces and interactions—with class, modernity, and sexuality. The representative figure here is perhaps Manet. Pound's criticism seems primarily aimed at the transparent Impressionism of Monet, whereas the Impressionism of *The Good Soldier* is surely rather the mediated version; its concern with the eye has more to do with treacherous glances, desire, how people look at and to each other, and what such looks reveal.

Pound's argument that Impressionism is flawed when "carried out of its due medium" (namely, paint) meant that he didn't like it in music, saying that it had "reduced us to such a dough-like state of receptivity that we have ceased to like concentration" ("Arnold Dolmetsch" 433). Yet he didn't seem to like it much even in paint. Thus he repeatedly criticized Futurism, somewhat cryptically, as merely "accelerated impressionism" (*Gaudier-Brzeska* 82, 90). Here too he was perhaps indebted to Ford, who, the previous month, had compared the Futurists to the French writers he thought of as quintessentially Impressionist: "The Futurist painters were doing very much what novelists of the type of Flaubert or short-story writers of the type of Maupassant aimed at. They gave you not so much the reconstitution of a crystallised scene in which all the figures were arrested—not so much that, as fragments of impressions gathered during a period of time, during a period of emotion, or during a period of travel" (*Critical Essays* 155). Pound's point is presumably that the Futurists still fetishize passive perception, but where the Impressionist painters were concerned with perceptions of light, color-field, and space, the Futurists are more interested in effects of energy and mechanical motion. Or perhaps he means that in making that shift they're again mixing up their media, carrying the cinematic out of its due medium and into paint:

> The age demanded an image
> Of its accelerated grimace
> . . . . . . . . . . . . . . . . . . . . . . .
> A prose kinema, not, not assuredly, alabaster.
> (*Hugh Selwyn Mauberley* 173-74)

Monet painted the effects of steam and steel, showing locomotives under the roof-canopy of the Gare Saint-Lazare (National Gallery, London, and

Art Institute of Chicago). Futurism, too, reveled in paintings of trains. Umberto Boccioni's 1911 *States of Mind I: The Farewells* (Museum of Modern Art, New York) has a looming locomotive plowing through a crowd which it disperses like the wake of a ship, or the steam from its funnel. Gino Severini's *Suburban Train Arriving in Paris* (Tate Modern, London) shows three separate plumes of smoke left by the locomotive at different points of its journey, as in the frames of a movie. Different though the techniques are, the Impressionist and Futurist versions are both concerned with the interplay of the substantial and the insubstantial, and with transience, though Futurism adds speed. Ford's poem "Finchley Road," about emerging from the underground at that London station, barely describes the train or the scene, but it sets up a contrast between an oppressive, overcast urban modernity and a nostalgic fantasy of a romantic past (*Selected Poems* 46-47). Pound's celebrated "In a Station of the Metro" works by a comparable juxtaposition, except that where Ford contrasts irreconcilabilities, Pound offers a metaphorical timeless oriental-sounding equivalent to his vision of haunting faces in the station. They are both concerned with perceptions, but of psychological states rather than visual appearances. And—crucially—Pound condenses Ford's more discursive, conventional stanzaic form down to a haiku-like pair of lines.

This may cast some doubt on the accuracy of Pound's recurrent objection to Fordian Impressionism as fixated on visual experience, the criticism that "His emotions make war on his will, but his perception of objects is excellent" (*Pound/Ford* 15). The essential point seems to be that Pound admires Ford's perceptiveness, but thinks he doesn't do enough with, or to, his perceptions. For Pound, Impressionism is simply an attempt to record or transcribe perceptions, and he thinks art, especially poetry, should do more.

Yet Ford's genius in a novel like *The Good Soldier* is to turn all these qualities Pound identifies against themselves. He uses the Jamesian technique of letting glimpses of the social surface lead to increasing knowledge of the specific gravity of things such as adultery, deception, sexual obsession, and madness. He uses the Conradian technique of letting a first person narrator's words say as much about the narrator as about his impressions, so that Ford's novel becomes a very effective, possibly very critical portrait of its ineffectual narrator, with his indecisions and confusions always under Ford's masterly control, as when he has Dowell describe his first impression of Edward Ashburnham's eyes in such a way as to make us wonder why they have made such an impression on him, why Edward has 'snapped up the gaze' not just of 'every woman' but of Dowell himself:

> When you looked at them carefully you saw that they were perfectly honest, perfectly straightforward, perfectly, perfectly stupid. But the brick pink of his complexion, running perfectly level to the brick pink of his inner eyelids, gave them a curious, sinister expression—like a mosaic of blue porcelain set in pink china. And that chap, coming into a room, snapped up the gaze of every woman in it, as dexterously as a conjurer pockets billiard balls. (29)

Pound's criticism about ineffectuality seems problematic at a more general level too. To put visual impressions into words is to do something to them, not to remain merely passive in relation to them. Though Ford is also thought to be the model for "the stylist" in *Hugh Selwyn Mauberley*, Pound doesn't allow that style is precisely the sign that perceptions have been worked up into something else.

It's not surprising that Pound's critique doesn't wash in the case of *The Good Soldier*, since Ford was just beginning the novel as Pound was voicing his objections. But he remained focused on Ford's contribution to poetics and relatively uninterested in the fiction that is Ford's strongest claim to major significance, and Ford teased him on that score: "Our distinguished colleague has always hated prose" (*Pound/Ford* 103).

However, around the moment of Imagism, Pound started relaxing his strictures against what he had diagnosed as "the flaw of impressionism" in March 1912, the same year in which Imagism was given its name, in the early autumn. He allows a place for the kind of visual verse he thinks Impressionism conduces to. One of his 1914 articulations of Vorticism identifies a "sort of poetry where painting or sculpture seems as if it were 'just coming over into speech'" (*Gaudier-Brzeska* 82).[6] And he starts distinguishing Fordian Impressionism from more problematic versions. In August and September 1913 Ford published an important essay in the Chicago magazine *Poetry* called "Impressionism—Some Speculations," which was revised into the preface to his *Collected Poems*, which came out later that year. In July 1914 Pound published an essay on Joyce in the *Egoist* which included this:

> I admire impressionist writers. English prose writers who haven't got as far as impressionism (that is to say, 95 per cent of English writers of prose and verse) are a bore.
>     Impressionism has, however, two meanings. . . .
>     There is a school of prose writers, and of verse writers for that matter, whose forerunner was Stendhal and whose founder was Flaubert. The followers of Flaubert deal in exact presentation. They are often so intent on exact presentation that they neglect intensity, selection, and concentration. They are perhaps the most clarifying and they have been perhaps the most beneficial force in modern writing.
>     There is another set, mostly of verse writers, who founded themselves not upon anybody's writing but upon the pictures of Monet.
>
> (*Literary Essays* 399-400)

Pound doesn't name the names of any of the practitioners of this evidently less admirable kind of Impressionism. But the examples he gives suggest that what he particularly objects to is a self-indulgent and inexact use of metaphor: "Thus one writer saw a picture by Monet and talked of 'pink pigs blossoming on a hillside,' and a later writer talked of 'slate-blue' hair and 'raspberry-coloured flanks'" (*Literary Essays* 400). In the way such things did with Pound, these became talismans for this critical argument. He had cited them in his "Prefatory Note" to "The Complete Poetical Works of T. E. Hulme," ironically appended to his own 1912 volume *Ripostes*, where, at least in the second case, he was thinking of French writing:

> the Impressionists who brought forth:
>     "Pink pigs blossoming upon the hillside";
> or of the Post-Impressionists who beseech their ladies to let down slate-blue hair over their raspberry-coloured flanks.
>     *Ardoise* rimed richly ah, richly and rarely rimed! with *framboise*.[7]
>
> (*Collected Shorter Poems* 251)

Ford's advocacy of Impressionism may well have led Pound to concede that some Impressionism was acceptable. (But note his qualification that even so it's too fixated on "exact presentation" at the expense of other poetic requirements.) And clearly by the time of his second review (in June 1914) of Ford's *Collected Poems*, which was titled "Mr. Hueffer and the Prose Tradition in Verse," Pound was placing Ford within the Flaubertian line of Impressionism, rather than the Monet line. Indeed, the year before Pound had seen Ford (as Ford saw himself) as an advocate of Flaubert, saying:

> I would rather talk about poetry with Ford Madox Hueffer than with any man in London. . . . Mr. Hueffer believes in an exact rendering of things. . . . He professes to prefer prose to verse. You would find his origins in Gautier or in Flaubert. He is objective. This school tends to lapse into description.
>
> ("Status rerum," qtd. in *Pound/Ford* 12)

This stress on exact description is where Pound's critique of Ford ultimately goes wrong. It's surely a quality of realism rather than Impressionism. By seeking to reduce Ford's writing to objective description, Pound obscures what's most striking—and strikingly Impressionist—about it: the evocations of subjectivities that spark around such descriptions. And that is the quality that Ford most owes to Flaubert, in whose work a description is always more than an exact transcription of the visual. The depiction at the end of *L'Education sentimentale*, for example, of the auction of Mme Arnoux's possessions is at once an exercise in pure material description—a cataloguing of bourgeois bric-a-brac—but also a lyrical evocation of the phantasmic quality of people's relationship with each other, and with material things, summoning up Frederic's absurd fondness for these commonplace objects because they remind him of his equally unrealistic, unrequited, love for Mme Arnoux.

As Pound's discussions with Ford helped him define his Imagist or Vorticist poetics, so, conversely, it's possible that Pound's early criticisms caused Ford to redefine *his* position. Certainly, it's only from 1913, and as he was about the begin *The Good Soldier*, that Ford begins to label himself explicitly as an Impressionist, first in that essay, "Impressionism—Some Speculations," then in another two-part essay of 1914 called "On Impressionism." In between, in September 1913, he published a slightly different version of the former, this time in the English magazine *The New Freewoman* (soon to become the *Egoist*), of which Pound had taken over the literary editorship.[8] This version was called "The Poet's Eye." Did Pound supply the title to keep up his attack on Impressionism as too ocular? Or was it Ford's title, defending the importance of Impressionism's visual attention? Either way, the phrase might be said to respond to Pound's criticism about Impressionism's eye flaw, and suggests that the debate was continuing, as we can perhaps also glimpse out of the corner of other eyes. The association of writing with the ocular is itself part of Ford's Flaubertian legacy. Flaubert had told Mlle Leroyer de Chantepie, "Tâchez de devenir un oeil," or "strive to become an eye" in Julian Barnes's translation.[9] Pound had published a poem in *Poetry* in August 1914 called "The Seeing Eye," a phrase that he may have been echoing from Ford, since it makes a striking appearance in the excerpt from *The Good Soldier* that had appeared in *Blast* that June under its original title, "The Saddest Story" (90).

Ford's essay "On Impressionism" is one of his most important, as well as one of his most explicit, statements of what he understands by the term. The first installment appeared in June 1914. Had Pound read it before writing his essay published that July on Joyce's *Dubliners*?[10] It's just possible. It's also conceivable that Ford showed Pound the manuscript, or discussed it with him, first. That's certainly how it had been a few months before, when Pound wrote to Dorothy Shakespear, "Ford [Madox Hueffer] has been in town for 24 hours, en route to Germany, and we rearranged his poems, & mucked about the preface of his 'Henry James,'"[11] showing that Pound not only was reading some of Ford's work before publication but, now a literary editor himself, was repaying the compliment or debt of being edited by Ford in the *English Review* in 1909-1910 (*Ezra Pound and Dorothy Shakespear* 256). It's also possible that Pound let Ford read a draft of his Joyce essay before that was published.

Whichever way any possible influence flows, it was already clear to Pound that Ford was identifying himself as Impressionist from at least the essays of the autumn of 1913. And the same month "On Impressionism" appeared saw the publication of Pound's second review of Ford's *Collected Poems* (the one locating him in the "Prose tradition" associated with the good Impressionism). That essay appeared in *Poetry* in the same issue as Ford's long poem, "On Heaven,"[12] which Pound had told Harriet Monroe was "the most important poem in the modern manner. The most important single poem that is," calling it "the best poem yet written in the 'twentieth-century fashion'" (*Selected Letters of Ezra Pound* 37). At the end of his review, however, Pound added this important footnote, which was omitted in T. S. Eliot's edition of Pound's *Literary Essays*:

> *Note.* Mr. Hueffer is not an *imagiste*, but an impressionist. Confusion has arisen because of my inclusion of one of his poems in the *Anthologie des Imagistes. E. P.*
>
>           ("Mr. Hueffer and the Prose Tradition in Verse" 120)[13]

If confusion really had arisen then, it certainly persisted about Ford's relation and relevance to Imagism, and a further reason is the fading of literary Impressionism from critical discourse. But it was evidently very much on Pound's mind in these years of intense aesthetic and literary ferment. And on Ford's too. He met Pound's assaults on Impressionism not just by sophisticating his own theory of it, but by telling Pound that the draft of what was then Canto 7 that he had sent Ford for comment was "a very beautiful piece of impressionism, as good as anything you have ever done" (*Pound/Ford* 63-64). Pound must have loved being told that. But it shows how, for this circle of writers, and especially for Pound and Ford, Impressionism continued to be the term through which or against which their poetics were defined.

## Notes

1. Ford's account in *It was the Nightingale* (220-21) is supported by Thomas C. Moser's analysis of the different handwriting in the manuscript (315-16n101), by Martin Stannard in his critical edition of *The Good Soldier*, and more recently by Aldington's letter to F. S. Flint, 4 July 1914, in Michael J. Copp's *Imagist Dialogues: Letters Between Aldington, Flint and Others.*

2. Aldington, "Vates, the Social Reformer" (Pound, *Des Imagistes* 59-61); Ford, "Fragments Addressed by Clearchus H. to Aldi" [an English poem written in classical Greek characters] (Pound, *Des Imagistes* 62). Ford's other poem in *Des Imagistes* is "In the Little Old Market-Place" (47-50).

3. "Ford Madox (Hueffer) Ford: Obit." David Moody sounds a note of skepticism about Pound's story, asking: "if the master felt the errors so strongly, why had he published four of those 'canzoni' in his review?" (112). Also see Peter Robinson 100. But there are over thirty other poems in the volume that may have got Ford on a roll.

4. Also see Saunders, "Literary Impressionism" and *Self Impression*.

5. See Saunders, *Self Impression* 371-419 on "Hugh Selwyn Mauberley" and life-writing.

6. See also "Vortex. Pound."

7. In "Pastiche. The Regional—IV," Pound was still making fun of his "discovery of the *neochromatist* who rhymed ardoise and framboise in his endeavour to persuade 'her' to let down her slate-coloured hair over her raspberry-coloured flanks" (220).

8. Pound told Alice Henderson in the 8-9 August 1913 letter that he would "control its literchure" (*Letters of Ezra Pound to Alice Corbin Henderson* 52).

9. Letter to Mlle Leroyer de Chantepie, 9 July 1861. *Correspondance* (Édition Louis Conard), quoted by Barnes.

10. "*Dubliners* and Mr. James Joyce."

11. 17 September 1913.

12. "Mr. Hueffer and the Prose Tradition in Verse," *Poetry* 4 (1914), 111-20. Reprinted as "The Prose Tradition in Verse" (*Literary Essays* 371-77).

13. The note also explains the title of the collection, which has puzzled some critics, indicating we are to understand the word "*Anthologie*" as implied.

## Works Cited

Aldington, Richard. *Life for Life's Sake*. New York: Viking, 1941. Print.

Armstrong, Paul. *The Challenge of Bewilderment: Understanding and Representation in James, Conrad, and Ford*. Ithaca: Cornell UP, 1987. Print.

Barnes, Julian. "Review of Jean-Benoît Guinot, *Dictionnaire Flaubert*. CNRS Éditions." *TLS* 4 June 2010: 26. Print.

Bretell, Richard, *Modern Art: 1851–1929: Capitalism and Representation*. Oxford: Oxford UP, 1999. Print.

Copp, Michael J. *Imagist Dialogues: Letters Between Aldington, Flint and Others*. Cambridge: Lutterworth Press, 2009. Print.

Ford, Ford Madox [Hueffer]. *Critical Essays*. Ed. Max Saunders and Richard Stang. Manchester: Carcanet, 2002. Print.

---. *The Good Soldier*. Ed. Max Saunders. Oxford: World's Classics-Oxford UP, 2012.

---. "Impressionism—Some Speculations." *Poetry* 2 (Aug. and Sept. 1913): 177-87, 215-25. Print.

---. *It was the Nightingale*. London: Heinemann, 1934. Print.

---. "On Impressionism." *Poetry and Drama* 2 (June and December 1914): 167-75, 323-34. Print.

---. "The Poet's Eye." *New Freewoman* 1 (1 and 15 Sept. 1913): 107-10, 126-27. Print.

---. "The Saddest Story." *Blast* 1 (1914): 87-97. Print.

---. *Selected Poems.* Ed. Max Saunders. Manchester: Carcanet, 1997. Print.

Katz, Tamar. *Impressionist Subjects: Gender, Interiority, and Modernist Fiction in England.* Urbana and Chicago: U of Illinois P, 2000. Print.

Matz, Jesse. *Literary Impressionism and Modernist Aesthetics.* Cambridge: Cambridge UP, 2001. Print.

Moody, A. David. *The Young Genius, 1885-1920.* Oxford: Oxford UP, 2007. Print. Vol. 1 of *Ezra Pound: Poet, A Portrait of the Man & His Work.* 1 vol. to date.

Moser, Thomas C. *The Life in the Fiction of Ford Madox Ford.* Princeton: Princeton UP, 1980. Print.

Pound, Ezra. "Arnold Dolmetsch." *Literary Essays.* 431-36. Print.

---. *Collected Shorter Poems.* London: Faber, 1984. Print.

---, ed. *Des Imagistes: An Anthology.* London and New York: The Poetry Bookshop and Albert and Charles Boni, 1914. Print.

---. "*Dubliners* and Mr. James Joyce." *Literary Essays* 399-402. Print.

---. *Gaudier-Brzeska.* New York: New Directions, 1974. Print.

---. *Hugh Selwyn Mauberley. Selected Poems.* Ed. T. S. Eliot. London: Faber, 1973. 171-87. Print.

---. *The Letters of Ezra Pound to Alice Corbin Henderson.* Ed. Ira B. Nadel. Austin: U of Texas P, 1993. Print.

---. *Literary Essays of Ezra Pound.* Ed. T. S. Eliot. London: Faber, 1954. Print.

---. "Mr. Hueffer and the Prose Tradition in Verse." *Poetry* 4 (June 1914): 111-20. Print.

---. "On Criticism in General." *Criterion* 1 (January 1923): 143-56. Print.

---. "Pastiche. The Regional—IV." *New Age* 25 (24 July 1919): 220. Print

---. "A Retrospect." *Literary Essays of Ezra Pound.* 3-14. Print.

---. *The Selected Letters of Ezra Pound.* Ed. D. D. Paige. New York: New Directions, 1971. Print.

---. *Selected Prose, 1909-1965.* Ed. William Cookson. New York: New Directions, 1973. Print.

---. "*Status rerum.*" *Poetry* 1 (January 1913): 123-27. Print.

---. "Vortex.Pound." *Blast* 1 (1914): 153-54. Print.

Pound, Ezra, and Ford Madox Ford. *Pound/Ford: The Story of a Literary Friendship: The Correspondence between Ezra Pound and Ford Madox Ford and Their Writings About Each Other.* Ed. Brita Lindberg-Seyersted. London: Faber & Faber, 1982. Print.

Pound, Ezra, and Dorothy Shakespear. *Ezra Pound and Dorothy Shakespear: Their Letters: 1909-1914.* Ed. Omar Pound and A. Walton Litz. London: Faber, 1985. Print.

Robinson, Peter. "'Written at Least as Well as Prose': Ford, Pound, and

Poetry." *Ford Madox Ford, Modernist Magazines, and Editing*. Ed. Jason
Harding. Amsterdam and Kenilworth, New Jersey: Rodopi, 2010. 99-
113. Print.

Saunders, Max. "Literary Impressionism." *A Companion to Modernist
Literature and Culture*. Ed. David Bradshaw and Kevin Dettmar. Oxford:
Blackwell, 2005. 204-11. Print.

---. *Self Impression: Life-Writing, Autobiografiction and the Forms of Modern
Literature*. Oxford: Oxford UP, 2010. Print.

# "Radiance to the White Wax": The Imagist Contradiction between *Logopoeia* and *Phanopoeia*

John Gery

Just glancing through *The Cantos of Ezra Pound* reveals how Pound's brief but intense engagement with the Imagist aesthetic remained with him the rest of his life, especially in his devotion to fusing immediate perception with design in his poetry. To trace almost randomly the imagery in early Cantos—from, say, "the first light, before ever dew was fallen" and "Through all the wood" where "the leaves are full of voices, / A-whisper, and the clouds bowe over the lake," to "the gray steps [that] lead up under the cedars" in Canto 3 (*The Cantos* 11) across "the valley . . . thick with leaves, with leaves" where "The sunlight glitters, glitters a-top, / Like a fish-scale roof," with "beneath it / Not a ray, not a slivver, not a spare disc of sunlight / Flaking the black, soft water" in Canto 4 (14), and then much later in Canto 49 through "a world . . . covered with jade / [where a] Small boat floats like a lanthorn, / The flowing water clots as with cold" (244), and then much further on to the "paw-flap, wave-tap" moving "toward limpidity" in Canto 110 (797)—is to enter a world dazzling with visual, aural, and tactile details, so richly textured, in fact, that individual passages often overwhelm the senses: "can you see with eyes of coral or turquoise / or walk with the oak's root?" Pound asks in Canto 110 (797). Only by looking closely at the "topaz against pallor of under-leaf / The lake waves

Canaletto'd / under blue paler than heaven, / the rock-layers arc'd as with a compass" (798), in Pound's paradisal vision, might we discover his "marble form in the pine wood, / The shrine seen and not seen" (*Cantos* 801).

As these lines suggest, in passage after passage, in Pound's poetry after Imagism—for all its "musical" phrases "not in sequence of a metronome" (Pound, *Literary* 3), for all its idiosyncratic diction—it consistently endeavors to give us "the direct treatment of the 'thing'" (*Literary* 3), that is, to convey an image, or what we might call a *Gestalt*, as precisely as "topaz against pallor of under-leaf," or as "rock-layers arc'd as with a compass." And despite the wide-ranging literary pastiche and craggy corners found throughout *The Cantos*, Pound never abandons his early ambition to render *exactly* what the eye sees and the ear hears. At first reading, then, Pound's Imagist technique seems nothing if not straightforward, initiating what was to become the prominent poetics behind the image-rich free verse that distinguishes much twentieth-century poetry from its predecessor. Yet pausing at the lines just cited in Canto 110, I cannot but wonder about the contradiction inherent there in what Pound writes about the pine wood, despite the clarity of the image: How *exactly* does the figure of "marble form in the pine wood" become a "shrine seen and *not* seen" (my italics)? How is it that (and this phenomenon recurs throughout *The Cantos*) the more precisely Pound describes an image, the less likely we are to see it *only* as an image and not also as a "shrine," icon, or even symbol of something else?

It is this contradiction between perception and cognition, implicit in the Imagist aesthetic, that I wish to explore. Given the "three principles" of composition that Pound devised with Richard Aldington and H.D. in 1912, what happens if and when the directive "to use absolutely no word that does not contribute to the presentation" conflicts with that for "the direct treatment of the 'thing' whether subjective or objective" (Pound *Literary* 3)? While these two rules may appear obviously correlated— namely, that one must, of course, use precise diction to present a subject directly—in practice they may not be so compatible. Pound himself, when he recasts Imagism somewhat differently years later in "How to Read" (1929) as comprising *melopoeia* (concerning a poem's "musical property"), *phanopoeia* (concerning the "casting of images upon the visual imagination"), and *logopoeia* (concerning prosody, or "'the dance of the intellect among words'"), asserts that *phanopoeia* can be "translated almost, or wholly, intact" from one language to another, whereas *logopoeia* "does not translate; though the attitude of mind it expresses may pass through a paraphrase" (*Literary* 25). In other words, although an image may be sufficiently nonverbal in character such that it can be rendered in virtually any language, much as we can readily identify imagery in visual artworks, even those by artists far removed from us in place or in time, prosody is subject to a more indigenous array of tonal variations unique to each language, making it arguable that no literature can be satisfactorily translated intact from one language into another.

Once Pound establishes in "How to Read" this rift between image and statement in poetry, he further characterizes *melopoeia* (the third element, linked to "the sequence of the musical phrase" in the Imagist manifesto) as also a "contrary current, a force tending often to lull, or to distract the reader from the exact sense of the language" (*Literary* 26). A poem's music, in his view, may counteract both its *phanopoeia* and its *logopoeia*. To be sure, the more we delve into all three of these principles of composition, the less reconcilable they become, despite Pound's authoritative posture when he first defined Imagism as a unified poetics in 1912. As Caroline Zilboorg has emphasized, in reflecting on Aldington's and H.D.'s collaborative contributions to Imagism, Aldington was to differentiate what H.D. and he were actually doing in their poems from Pound's theorizing. Zilboorg contends that, contrary to the prevalent criticism that Aldington's early poems "fail to embody" the "principles behind H.D.'s first mature poems," "it is more likely that these early modernist theories of verse were developed by H.D. with Aldington" (41). Zilboorg then cites a letter from Aldington to Herbert Read where he discounts any debt to Imagist theory when he writes, "Hulme=0," and argues "that imagism, as written by H.D. and me, was purely our own invention and was not an attempt to put a theory into practice. The 'school' was Ezra's invention" (Zilboorg 41). In other words, to the extent that the theory and practice were distinct ventures, any contradictions in Pound's doctrine need not, nor did, detract from its practice by Aldington, H.D., and the other Imagists.

Nevertheless, in exploring the specific contradictions between the Imagist image (*phanopoeia*) and what Pound later calls the "most tricky and undependable mode" of *logopoeia* (*Literary* 25), I want to consider its manifestation in several Imagist poems. As Thomas Grieves defines it, *logopoeia* "focuses on the insides of the poem, on matters of content and meaning" (103), yet this element of poetry, its sensible or thematic aspect, according to Pound, "cannot possibly be contained in plastic or in music" (*Literary* 25). So how, then, can a reader derive a poem's sentiment or attitude without corrupting the image? Looking at specific instances in T. E. Hulme's "Above the Dock," Aldington's "Images," and H.D.'s "Song," I want to locate where in each poem its sense may *detract* from its image, in order to demonstrate how, in fact, precise language can disrupt an image, thereby creating the very tension that discloses "meaning," even as it may also render Imagism as a poetics *imprecise*.

Despite Aldington's disregard of his influence on his own poetry, T. E. Hulme commands a central place in the genesis of Imagism, stemming from his skeptical view of the Romantics' divination of a subject and his advocacy for "dry, small words" (Thacker 50).[1] Like Pound, Hulme was an unhesitating proponent of sometimes contradictory principles. For instance, on the one hand, he declared himself a Classicist by virtue of his allegiance to a concrete language (especially in poetry), while on the other, he considered analogical or figurative thought as primordial to the predominantly logical heterodoxy of his contemporaries, such as Bertrand Russell and the Logical Positivists.[2] (In one analogy, Hulme describes poetry as a pedestrian traversing a landscape and seeing its signposts, in contrast to prose, which he sees as a train passing over the terrain in its aim toward a single destination [Edwards 32].) Often writing in a fragmented style that anticipates the Pound of, say, *Jefferson and/or Mussolini* and *Guide to Kulchur*, Hulme emphasizes the primacy of the emotional subconsciousness, even as he argues for the image (or physiological perception) as a priori to language; language, by contrast, he considers inevitably (if not hopelessly) abstract.

In the case of Hulme's "Above the Dock"—a seeming paradigm of an Imagist poem that (like Pound's "In a Station of the Metro") employs juxtaposition, spare diction, "direct treatment of the thing," and a rhythm skewed against its own rhyme—the poem, thematically speaking, ultimately hinges on a single word, though almost indiscernibly:

Above the quiet dock in midnight,
Tangled in the tall mast's corded height,
Hangs the moon. What seemed so far away
Is but a child's balloon, forgotten after play. (Pratt 63)

Hulme's title and first line neutrally set the scene, as the word "quiet," for instance, fixes the poem's mood without judgment. The rhymes of *midnight/ height* and *away/play* are off-kilter, in metrical accent in the first case and the number of metrical feet per line in the second. The image of the moon hanging "tangled" in the ship's mast (again using evocative internal, yet irregular rhyme and assonance) creates a vivid image, even without directly mentioning a ship or specifying its height; this image Hulme then contrasts with an image of the child's balloon evidently ensnared "after play," not in the mast's "corded height," presumably, but as it would be in a tree (though no tree is mentioned). In a sentence of only sixteen words, Hulme manages to project not two but three images, the sky with the moon in it above the dock, the moon "tangled" in a ship's mast, and a child's balloon in a tree.

Yet finally, the *sense* of this figurative glimpse of the moon emerges in the least concrete of the poem's phrases, "What seemed so far away / Is but," a clause which 1) places the image itself partly in the past, 2) reveals the image as merely an impression that "seemed" one thing but "is" actually something else, and most significantly, 3) portrays the image as *diminished* by this revelation: the moon observed as a grandly distant object turns out to be "but" a child's plaything. The adverbial use of "but" here divulges the poem's sense, or the "attitude of mind" which Pound argues can be conveyed through translation only by paraphrase. Using "but" in this manner, not only does Hulme domesticate the moon, but he undermines its status as an astronomical, divine, or even astrological source of power. As Paul Edwards observes, here (as in his poem "Mana Aboda"), "where a Romantic poet would try to make familiar things seem important by comparing them with the moon or sea, Hulme reverses the effect and makes infinite things seem small and homely" (36).[3] Robert Ferguson, in considering the same metaphor, goes so far as to suggest that it expresses Hulme "consciously taking leave of his [troubled] childhood" (40) in his readiness to accept adulthood. I don't know that I agree with Ferguson's psychoanalytic reading, but such an interpretation further underscores how easy it is for the single word "but" here to shape an otherwise indeterminate comparison; to read Hulme's balloon as metonymic of childhood—though not as a Wordsworthian "spot of time," neither as a "concrete thing"—is to acknowledge the poet's subtle manipulation of his material, even of his perception of the world itself. Put another way, Pound's post-Hulmean Imagist directive, "to use no word that does not contribute to the presentation," might well advise removing "but" here, and even Hulme's verb, "Is," could be deleted (making line four a regular iambic pentameter line, if a sentence fragment). However, would not removing "but"—and with it the poem's "emotion" (or bias) about the moon in the ship's rigging—also flatten its tension, its deconstruction of the speaker's mood? Or would a direct juxtaposition of its two images more forcefully, more accurately, more *concretely*, convey the mood its "small, dry words" invoke? In other words, does approaching a *phanopoeic* ideal in a poem such as "Above the Dock" necessarily undermine its *logopoeic* power?

Like Hulme's poem, Richard Aldington's "Images," read either as a gathering of short poems or as a sequence, also reveals conflicts between the *phanopoeic* and the *logopoeic*. One telling difference in Aldington's technique is his explicit use of similes in three of the poem's six numbered sections. But in the other three sections, as in "Above the Dock," the poem creates juxtapositions through "to be" verbs: (III) "a roe-yellow moon in a pale sky / . . . / Art thou to me"; (V) the red deer "are high on the mountain, / [and] are beyond the last pine trees"; and (VI) "The flower . . . / Is soon filled" (Pratt 102-03). Indeed, the use of passive verbs can result in the kind of grammatical stasis that I suspect later irked Pound away from Imagism towards Vorticism. But another difference between Aldington's and Hulme's poems concerns how Aldington's sequence directly addresses its reader, a beloved variously referred to as "exquisite one," as one seen as a moon, as one both still and trembling, and as one who, upon returning, can relieve the speaker's mind filled with misgiving. In short, Aldington deliberately strains his language to name and to engage the beloved, therein displaying, perhaps, the most subjective of all human emotions: desire. Yet by using these apostrophes, he categorizes his feelings for the beloved, an act that renders his emotions ultimately as "objective," as *shared*.[4] How is it possible, in this case, for the poet to provide a "direct treatment of the thing" when the "insides of the poem," to use Grieve's phrase, require such a complex, double-edged trope of the self?

Both Aldington and H.D. in many of their Imagist poems, I believe, do just that—that is, reconcile the *phanopoeic* with the *logopoeic*, despite their incongruity. In Part I of Aldington's "Images," for instance,

> Like a gondola of green scented fruits
> Drifting along the dank canals at Venice,

> You, O exquisite one,
> Have entered my desolate city. (Pratt 102)

The key term is "desolate." Yes, the beloved may be "exquisite," a subjective, abstract modifier, but what shapes Aldington's otherwise vivid simile in the image of the gondola loaded down with (or even comprised of) "scented fruits" is how it closes with the beloved (as a boat!) entering "my desolate city." Whereas the canals in Venice are "dank," an olfactory detail, "desolate" conveys the *sense*, rather than the *sensation*, of both the city's and the speaker's condition. By way of contrast, Part IV reads,

> As a young beech-tree on the edge of a forest
> Stands still in the evening,
> Yet shudders through all its leaves in the light air
> And seems to fear the stars
> So are you still and so tremble. (Pratt 102-03)

Here the beech-tree is said to "shudder through all its leaves," while it only "*seems* to fear the stars" (my italics), as the poet admits to the gap between the tree itself and his own personification of it. Yet the beloved in the final line embodies both what the tree is observed to *be* (namely, "still") and what the tree is observed to *do* ("shudder" or "tremble"). In this simply stated, yet detailed juxtaposition of vehicle and tenor, Aldington adds a phrase ("seems to fear") that does not, in fact, contribute to the direct presentation of the image, yet he *is* precise in rendering a direct presentation of the "thing" (the tree, the beloved) *as it functions in the poet's mind*. Adrian Barlow attributes this exactness in Aldington's technique to the influence of haiku and Greek poetry when he remarks how such lines "relocate the sculptures, deities, and landscapes of [Aldington's] Hellenist imagination ironically in the contemporary city" (10), as the poet transposes what he imagines onto what he sees before him (10).

In the best sense, after all, the Imagist directives do not mandate a formula but aim (even for Aldington and H.D.) to restore to poetry a more closely aligned, if not an entirely seamless, link between the signifier and the signified, to use Saussurean terms. If a poet violates any of the three "rules" (which, Pound claims in a letter to Harriet Monroe, he originally offered to her with "A Few Don'ts" as something to include in rejection letters to "neophytes" and would-be contributors to *Poetry* [*Selected Letters* 18, 78-79]), it may be necessary to do so, in order to strike a balance between an implied metaphor's vehicle and tenor. In Part IV of Aldington's "Images," the stillness of the beloved as much informs the image of the beech tree (*phanopoeically*) as the image of the beech tree informs our conception of the beloved's vulnerability, a vulnerability the poet portrays with . . . with what? Affection? Desire? Sympathy? This question of the poet's self-interested motivation here opens the Pandora's box of most poetry about love and remains provocatively ambiguous, as image and feeling remain at a stand-off, yoked together yet suspended from each other.

H.D.'s "Song" provides an even better example of the delicate point in an Imagist metaphor where the *logopoeic* detracts from the *phanopoeic* but does so purposefully, as implicit to, if not spelled out by, Pound's Imagist theory. Composed as two sentences of one strophe each (nine and eight lines), the poem portrays the beloved, as in Part IV of "Images," through its intricately woven syntax, rhythm, rhyme, assonance, and lineation. Like Hulme and Aldington, H.D. also relies on passive verbs in both strophes:

> You are as gold
> as the half-ripe grain
> that merges to gold again,
> as white as the white rain
> that beats through
> the half-opened flowers
> of the great flower tufts
> thick on the black limbs
> of an Illyrian apple bough.
>
> Can honey distill such fragrance
> as your bright hair—
> for your face is as fair as rain,
> yet as rain that lies clear
> on white honey-comb,
> lends radiance to the white wax,
> so your hair on your brow
> casts light for a shadow. (*Collected* 133; Pratt 92[5])

If not consciously, certainly with gusto, H.D.'s first strophe echoes for me Robert Burns's "My Love is like a red, red rose" (99), although H.D. qualifies her simile, as Sappho might, thereby insinuating that the beloved is far from generic, but is specifically "gold / as the *half-ripe* grain / that merges to gold again" (my italics), in an image as singular as William Carlos Williams's wheelbarrow "glazed with rain / water" in the aftermath of a storm (Pratt 106); the reference also recalls seasonal references used in haiku. In addition, the quality of white is very specific, likened to that rain that "beats through / the half-opened flowers" found on "the black limbs / of an Illyrian apple bough," as the poet turns botanist: A reader may need a field guide to ascertain exactly the quality of whiteness attributed to the beloved here. The "treatment of the 'thing'" could not be more direct, more than even Pound might demand.

In the second strophe, however, the *logopoeic* turns the mind away from the strictly *phanopoeic*, and the difference in expression is all: H.D. asks a question yet uses no question mark. The slant rhymes, which in strophe one are pronounced (*grain/again/rain, flowers/bough*), are now muted (*hair/clear, fragrance/rain, brow/shadow*). Even the grammar becomes slippery. Yet because of the visual accuracy of the first strophe, the poem remains focused on its vehicle, on the conceit for the beloved's attributes (goldness, whiteness, openness). "Can honey distill such fragrance / As your bright hair?" the poet asks, then follows with an apparent explanation for her question: "for your face is as fair as rain," an image that itself could close the strophe, with its depiction of the beloved's face left to "speak" for itself, *phanopoeically*, as it were. But here H.D. shifts into the *logopoeic*, the "insides" of the poem, the sense behind the sensation, by way of a subsidiary metaphor to modify the primary one: The rain to which the beloved's face is implicitly compared is that rain which "lies clear / on white honey-comb," as the poet gauges the quality of this particular type of rain that manages to "beat through / the half-opened flowers," this rain that "lends radiance to the white wax" on the honey-comb. The term "radiance" here simultaneously conveys *both* the sensation and the sense of the water. As this poem's vital word, "radiance" *means* as it also *describes*, therein defying Archibald MacLeish's dictum that "A poem should not mean / But be" (Pratt 173). In a style marked by, as Cyrena N. Pondrom describes it, "the total absence of words which describe an emotion or state of being" but which instead "presents an action which embodies a mood" (95), H.D.

nonetheless reveals a powerfully felt awe and desire for her subject.

But then she turns this conception back to the image, to present the beloved yet one more time, as one whose hair (gold and white) "casts light for a shadow," creating a remarkable impression of radiance itself that invests the beloved with a kind of divinity, even as it suggests the speaker's own passion. As an Imagist, H.D. could not be more direct, both objectively and subjectively, yet her feeling takes over the poem entirely, as it leaves us with a "radiance" not fixed on the image but emanating from the immediate into the realm of the speaker's desire. More than strip the poem of excesses in sense, more than root it too austerely in its imagery, H.D.'s precisely expressed *im*precision, her subtly wrought inflection of the *logopoeic* into the *phanopoeic*, of "radiance to the white wax," is really what Pound discovered in her work, I think, as the premise for Imagism.

In his 1913 essay "The Wisdom of Poetry," written while he was still fully engaged with Imagism, Pound comments on the poet's function in relation to truth: "As the poet was, in ages of faith, the founder and emender of all religions, so, in ages of doubt, is he the final agnostic; that which the philosopher presents as truth, the poet presents as that which appears as truth to a certain sort of mind under certain conditions" (*Selected Prose* 361). Is not the Imagist directive, beyond its emphasis on concision and melodic prosody, to devise a poetry that, in treating a "thing" directly, presents it "as that which *appears* [my italics] as truth to a certain sort of mind under certain conditions," so that what finally "contributes to the presentation" may require a "but" (Hulme), a "desolate" or a "seems to fear" (Aldington), and a "radiance" (H.D.), despite such words not "casting an image on the visual imagination" (*Literary* 25)? "The poet," Pound adds, "is consistently agnostic in this; that he does not postulate his ignorance as a positive thing. . . . He grinds an axe for no dogma" (*Selected Prose* 361). This richly layered skepticism, as Pound conceives of it, anticipates exactly the paradox of "the marble form in the pine wood" Pound regards as "the shrine seen and not seen" in Canto 110 fifty years after Imagism. And it is precisely because of this paradoxical collaboration of sensation and sense in Imagist poetics that its legacy endures.

## Notes

1. For a thorough account of Hulme's modernist thinking about language, especially of

the dichotomy of the Classical and Romantic senses of poetic language, see Thacker 44-53. For instance, in comparing Hulme's "Notes on Language and Style" (where Hulme writes, "Dead things not men as the material for art" [27]), Thacker not only quotes Pound's comment in a 1915 letter to Harriet Monroe that "Language is made out of concrete things. General expressions in non-concrete terms are a laziness; they are talk, not art, not creation" (Pound, *Selected Letters* 49), but he further cites Ludwig Wittgenstein's *Tractatus* where "Wittgenstein writes that thoughts are expressed in propositions, and propositions are composed of 'simple signs,' the primitive building blocks for language. . . . Crucially, Wittgenstein writes that the 'requirement that simple signs be possible is the requirement that sense be determinate' (3.23). In order for the ambiguities of language to be overcome words must be seen as 'simple signs,' 'small, dry things' that picture and resemble objects in the world" (Thacker 47). Such thinking prompted Pound's advocacy for both the economy and concreteness of poetic language (even before he had read Ernest Fenollosa).

2. See Thacker 39-42.

3. Ed Block, Jr., argues further how Hulme's juxtaposition of the moon and the balloon imagery "changes the spatio-temporal coordinates" and "reveals its modernity in the particularly unapologetic way it leaves the reader to fill in the empty space left in the incongruity of the two observations, [since] the 'perceiver' in the poem has withdrawn," thereby offering "a pattern of possible perceptions which will overcome the pragmatic cast of perception and language" (165). However, what I mean to suggest is that the abstract phrase, "What seemed so far away / Is but," is less objective, less open-ended, than Block implies.

4. As Helen Carr points out, the term "objective" used in the first principle of the Imagist manifesto Pound probably took from Ford Madox Ford, whereas "direct" was "one of Hulme's watchwords" (492). Despite their being yoked by Pound, this distinction in derivation is significant, I think, in terms of reading the expression of emotions in Aldingon's and, especially, H.D.'s Imagist poetry. Discussing the implicit subjective-objective dichotomy in this principle, Ethan Lewis argues, "Pound's faith in intuition, in the existence of facts accessible to all via 'accurate,' 'clear' reporting, denotes a world outside the self to which separate selves have access. Subjective impressions number among realities to be objectively recorded, thence shared" (278). But Carr suggests a far less formulaic notion of the goal of Imagism when she writes how, in following Hulme's lead, "capturing an emotion directly had always been Pound's aim" (482), in that he "wanted poetry 'free from emotional slither,' in other words, not without emotion, but the emotion, as he says in his introduction to Cavalcanti, must be 'exact'" (Carr 492).

5. In Pratt's third edition of *The Imagist Poem*, lines 11-12 begin with upper case letters ("As" and "For"), but since that is the case in neither H.D.'s *Collected Poems* nor the first edition of Pratt's anthology, I am using the earlier version here. See H.D. 133, Pratt, *The Imagist Poem* (1963 edition) 67.

## Works Cited

Barlow, Adrian. "A Reading of Aldington's Poetry." *Richard Aldington: Reappraisals*. Ed. Charles Doyle. Victoria, BC: U of Victoria, 1990. 7-25. Print.

Block, Ed, Jr. "Lyric Voice and Reader Response: One View of the Transition to Modern Poetics." *Twentieth Century Literature* 42.2 (1978): 154-168. Print.

Burns, Robert. *Representative Poems of Robert Burns*. Ed. Charles Lane Handson. Boston: Ginn and Company, 1930. Print.

Carr, Helen. *The Verse Revolutionaries: Ezra Pound, H.D. and the Imagists*. London: Jonathan Cape, 2009. Print.

Comentale, Edward P., and Andrzej Gasiorek. "Introduction: On the Significance of a Hulmean Modernism." Comentale and Gasiorek 1-22.

Comentale, Edward P., and Andrzej Gasiorek, eds. *T. E. Hulme and the Question of Modernism*. Burlington, VT: Ashgate, 2006. Print.

Edwards, Paul. "The Imagery of Hulme's Poetry and Notebooks." Comentale and Gasiorek 23-38.

Ferguson, Robert. *The Short Sharp Life of T. E. Hulme*. London: Allen Lane/ Penguin, 2002. Print.

Grieve, Thomas F. *Ezra Pound's Early Poetry and Poetics*. Columbia: U of Missouri P, 1997. Print.

H.D. *Collected Poems, 1912-1944*. Ed. Louis L. Martz. New York: New Directions, 1983. Print.

Hulme, T. E. *The Collected Writings of T. E. Hulme*. Ed. Karen Csengeri. Oxford: Clarendon, 1994. Print.

Lewis, Ethan. "Imagism." *Ezra Pound in Context*. Ed. Ira B. Nadel. Cambridge: Cambridge UP, 2010. 274-84. Print.

Pondrom, Cyrena N. "H.D. and the Origins of Imagism." *Signets: Reading H.D.* Ed. Susan Stanford Friedman and Rachel Blau Duplessis. Madison: U of Wisconsin P, 1991. 85-109. Print.

Pound, Ezra. *The Cantos of Ezra Pound*. New York: New Directions, 1995. Print.

---. *Literary Essays of Ezra Pound*. Ed. T. S. Eliot. New York: New Directions, 1935. Print.

---. *Personae: The Shorter Poems of Ezra Pound*. Rev. ed. Ed. Lea Baechler and A. Walton Litz. New York: New Directions, 1990. Print.

----. *Selected Letters, 1907-1941*. Ed. D. D. Paige. New York: New Directions, 1950. Print.

----. *Selected Prose, 1909-1965*. Ed. William Cookson. New York: New Directions, 1973. Print.

Pratt, William, ed. *The Imagist Poem: Modern Poetry in Miniature*. 3rd ed. New Orleans: U of New Orleans P, 2008. Print. Rpt. of The Imagist Poem: Modern Poetry in Miniature. Rev. ed. Ashland, OR: Story Line

P, 2001.

---, ed. *The Imagist Poem: Modern Poetry in Miniature*. New York: Dutton, 1963. Print.

Thacker, Andrew. "A Language of Concrete Things: Hulme, Imagism and Modernist Theories of Language." Comentale and Gasiorek 39-55.

Wittengenstein, Ludwig. *Tractatus Logico-Philosophicus*. Trans. D. F. Pears and B. F. McGuiness. London: Routledge and Kegan Paul, 1961. Print.

Zilboorg, Caroline. "H.D.'s Influence on Richard Aldington." *Richard Aldington: Reappraisals*. Ed. Charles Doyle. Victoria, BC: U of Victoria, 1990. 26-44. Print.

# The Formalistic Grounds for William Carlos Williams's Critique of Imagism

J. T. Welsch

The deceptively unadorned images of William Carlos Williams's early poetry, such as his famous "figure 5 in gold" or "red wheelbarrow," are often introduced to new readers as straightforward examples of Imagism. However, beyond his loose affiliation and inclusion in the first Imagist anthology of 1914, Williams's own opinion of the movement was increasingly negative. In order to move past what seems oversimplified understanding of both Williams's poetic principles and those of Imagism, I would like to re-examine the specific terms of Williams's critique within the wider context of his development. Before getting into the content of this critique, however, it may prove helpful to sketch out some of the relevant historical points regarding Williams's brief "official" involvement with and then disengagement from his friend Ezra Pound's version of Imagism. In this way, we can move from the history, which may be more familiar, into some broader ideas regarding Williams's poetics before finally considering the relationship between these two.

In all of this, one of my main points of emphasis is the retrospective nature of Williams's account, which is to say, the way he only begins to articulate his negative characterization of Imagism as a superseded historical movement—or "dead mode," as he calls it—in comments from the late 1930s or early 1940s onwards.[1] The critique itself appears to follow from earlier expressions in which his own poetics remains too unformed to pit confidently against the movement. Therefore, I think it would be a mistake to read these scattered later remarks as a true memory of Williams's reaction at the time, or as a rationalization for his break with the movement. Rather, any sense of a deliberate break expressed in those later comments, in terms of poetics or poetic ideology, appears to be itself a kind of backward construction onto a transition which was clearly rather drawn-out and haphazard for Williams. In this regard, I argue that in his later attitude, to some extent, we see Williams using Imagism as a synecdoche for his earlier self, or as a means to externalize and distance himself from what he considers a less poetically mature position—a position in which, with the benefit of hindsight, he saw his immature work merely following or imitating that of Pound outright.[2] In this way, these few pointed critical remarks from the 1940s represent a somewhat narcissistic conflation of his own personal development with that of early twentieth-century American poetry, in so far as he retrospectively fills in gaps, anachronistically criticizing Imagism and/or his younger self for not having known better, or not having known what he had gathered in the intervening years and through various other influences.

Returning to that earlier moment of Imagism as objectively as we can, the beginning of the end of Williams's commitment to "orthodox" Imagism (if there is such a thing) appears broadly framed by his relationship with Pound. Pound's poetic, philosophical, and personal influence on Williams was at its height between 1910, when Williams visited his old university friend in London, and 1914-1915, when Williams began his involvement with the Others group in New York. Of course, this period also corresponds roughly to the period of Pound's own direct involvement with Imagism as a movement. Therefore, I would summarize Williams's official allegiance as beginning when Pound included his poem "Postlude" in the original anthology and ending when Pound left the helm, as it were, to Amy Lowell. If nothing else, Williams makes his loyalties quite clear in a heated correspondence with Lowell in the autumn of 1916, where he informs her in no uncertain terms that "aside from what you stole from Pound, your venture is worthless" (*Selected Letters* 37). Lowell, for her part, offered several times to meet with Williams, ostensibly hoping to work through their differences, but Williams flatly refused. Nevertheless, when Lowell forwarded Williams's incensed letter to John Gould Fletcher in

England, along with her account of what she called "an exchange of arms" with Williams, she sounded as much disappointed as offended. Williams seemed "sincere," she thought, but unfortunately was "still enthralled to Ezra," whom she held in slightly lesser regard (Mariani 788n62).

Lowell is half right here, I would argue, insofar as Williams's loyalty to Pound does partly account for his defensiveness. On the other hand, another good part of Williams's self-assuredness (which is not to say characteristic indignation) towards Lowell is not only based on his disconnection from the movement, but also on having finally found an artistic community of his own, and in his own backyard. Williams had published only two small books at this point, one of which he had paid for himself and promptly disowned, the other of which Pound had arranged printing in London.[3] By his own account, Williams remained desperate in New Jersey for a "vortex" like the one Pound had shown him in London (*Recognizable Image* 57). Although Williams's affiliation with the Others group in New York was the product of his own volition, the gatekeeper for Williams's new community turned out to be Alfred Kreymborg, who had printed *Des Imagistes* for Pound, but who had no lasting allegiance to the group otherwise. When Pound sent Kreymborg the manuscript in New York, he suggested that Williams get in touch with Kreymborg too (Pound, *Letters* 27).

Aside from coming at a time in his early career when Williams was anxious for contact on his side of the Atlantic, the introduction to Kreymborg's circle also happily coincided with a genuine revolution (or various intermingled revolutions) in the visual arts, which had already caught Williams's attention. The invasion of the new continental art— which found an eager ally in the native avant-garde, and of which Williams wanted part—made its first splash at the Armory Show in 1913, the year before *Des Imagistes*. Williams scholars and Williams himself frequently cite this infamous exhibition as one of several crucial epiphanies in the course of his early development, particularly the moment when the poet stood before Marcel Duchamp's scandalous "Nude Descending a Staircase, No. 2" and "laughed out loud, with relief" (*Autobiography* 134). Within two years, through Kreymborg's *Others* magazine—a few issues of which Williams was allowed to edit—through the weekend retreats to the budding artists' colony at Grantwood, and through related artistic circles via Alfred Stieglitz's *291* gallery, Williams was able to immerse himself in the community he had longed for, even making the acquaintance of

Duchamp himself. Pound may have arranged the introduction, but the zeal with which Williams threw himself into this world provided in return the confidence and independence that, I argue, lie behind his later disavowal of Imagism and his earlier period. The *Others* journal also meant Williams was no longer completely reliant on Pound's influence over Harriet Monroe, the editor of *Poetry*, to get his poems into print.[4] Whether or not the relatively obscure *Others* ever posed any real challenge to the poetry establishment at the time, it offered enough of a cause and clearly gave Williams a ground from which to rebuff Lowell's olive branch.

Following Bram Dijkstra's seminal 1969 study of Williams's visual arts influences, various critics have quite rightly read the decade after the Armory Show as a time of more fundamental changes in Williams's poetic practice and thinking about art generally. The relationship between this shift and the legacy of Imagism has occasionally been a point of interest as well. Dijkstra himself slightly underplays distinctions between the two by suggesting that the tenets of Imagism—regardless of Pound's or F. S. Flint's insistence that they had "nothing at all in common" with the Post-Impressionist schools—were more or less repeated in what Williams learned from the new painting (24). Perhaps taking his lead from Williams's later, more directly expressed feelings about Imagism, however, Dijkstra does concede that "the intensity of avant-garde activity and theorizing in New York beginning with the Armory Show left Imagism a rather unexciting and even redundant bone to chew on for poets like Williams" (25).

Nevertheless, without ignoring the intensity of these few years for Williams, I would highlight again the time it took for him to digest these visual arts influences—a full decade if we accept the common mark of 1923's *Spring and All* as the first full articulation of Williams's post-Imagist, cubist-inflected principles in its prose sections and as the first full exhibition of these ideas in its breakthrough poems.[5] Again, even with that marker, as I have mentioned, it was nearly a further twenty years before Williams would make the comments with which I am concerned, in which the lessons of those decades are brought into a deferred critique of Imagism.

This last point is worth stressing, as we move toward a reconsideration of Williams's post-Imagistic poetics: thirty years after the fact, the principles developed in the decade between the Armory Show and *Spring and All*, and further refined through his association with the Objectivists in the early 1930s, become the very terms of his anachronistic critique of

Imagism. These terms are scattered in comments from the 1940s and 1950s, once artistic maturity and reputation affords Williams such self-assured hindsight, and they seem to focus on two subtly interrelated concepts: namely, structure and a relationship between the self and reality through art. Structure, or a general structurality, is the key, and Williams is most adamant in a talk at Harvard in 1941, declaring that Imagism "lost its place finally because as a form it completely lacked structural necessity" ("Basis of Poetic Form" 24). In another lecture from 1948, he repeats: "Imagism was not structural: that was the reason for its disappearance" (*Selected Essays* 283).

Williams can be frustrating in his refusal to define his use of vague catchwords like "structure," but the most basic familiarity with Williams's poetry makes clear that he is not lamenting Imagism's failure to employ traditional poetic forms. Rather, the definition in which I am most interested is his more abstract philosophical idea of *structure* as the foundation of the poem's very existence, or what he refers to as its "actuality." Thus, for Williams, Imagism's chief shortcoming seems to be that in its "direct treatment of the 'thing'"—i.e., some "thing" outside the poem—its tenets fail to address the poem's own structural integrity (or "structural necessity," as he says), by which the poem itself is experienced as an object or "thing" of equal "being." In this way, Williams's ideal poem exists as an equally structural object in its own right. Rather than "treating" some other extra-linguistic thing, it is the thing: "not realism, but reality itself" (*Imaginations* 114).

Although Williams's insistence on the poem's object-like "actuality" might appear to belong quintessentially to his and Louis Zukofsky's Objectivist principles, it has its roots in the formalistic Cubist and Futurist influences of that period immediately following Williams (and Pound's) Imagist interlude. Apollinaire's 1913 article "Les Peintres Cubistes" had been reprinted in *The Little Review* in 1922 while Williams was writing *Spring and All*, and in that book he echoes Apollinaire's insistence on the need to replace the classical notion of mimesis, or what Williams paraphrases as "the falseness of attempts to 'copy' nature," with a conception of the work of art as a spatial and temporal entity in its own right, which might "replace not the form but the reality of experience with its own" (*Imaginations* 107, 117). The best and most timeless compositions, he concludes in *Spring and All*, "have as their excellence an identity with life since they are as actual" (*Imaginations* 101). In 1932's *Novelette* as well, he aspires to "the works of any painter who is no longer content to 'represent' but lives to 'create' as they say, to advance, that is, the concept of the real, the actual" (*Imaginations* 271).

In terms of method, Williams goes further by relating the conceptual emphasis on the poem's structural actuality to a practical emphasis on the material of the work of art, advocating an identity or parity between that work and the physical reality beyond its frame. Towards the end of his *Autobiography*, Williams fondly recalls "the years when the painters following Cézanne began to talk of sheer paint: a picture a matter of pigments upon a piece of cloth stretched on a frame" (380). For Williams, this foregrounding of materiality also goes hand-in-hand with the foregrounding of structurality suggested by Kandinsky's ideal of "the constructive dispersal of the fragments over the canvas" in his treatise *Concerning the Spiritual in Art*, which Williams quotes from enthusiastically in his Prologue to 1920's *Kora in Hell* (Kandinsky 39). And for the poem, the equivalent of dispersed material fragments—such as those in Duchamp's *Nude Descending a Staircase*, which a New York journalist jokingly described as "an explosion in a shingle factory"—is, as Williams often reminds us, the words themselves (Wilson, Pilgrim, and Tashjian 211).

As with Kandinsky's conception of the work of art, Williams's ideal poem is an object constituted not only by the materiality of its "canvas" (print or sound, in the case of poetry), but by the constructive dispersal itself, by "the spaces between words and their configurations"—in other words, by its total structure. To this formalistic end, it is not Ezra Pound but Gertrude Stein, whose writing on art Williams read in Alfred Stieglitz's *Camera Work*, who provided the primary model, having "stressed as [Georges] Braque did paint, words" themselves (*Embodiment* 22). Yet the basic principle is the same: the words themselves become like Cézanne's sheer paint by virtue of their constructive dispersal, by a structural necessity never specified by Imagist tenets prescribing an economy of language, or mere "technical hygiene," as Hugh Kenner famously defined it (178).

Williams also admits that Imagism "had been useful in ridding the field of verbiage" (*Autobiography* 264) through its insistence on "no superfluous word, no adjective, which does not reveal something" or "absolutely no word that does not contribute to the presentation," as Pound rephrases the dictum in "A Retrospect" (3-4). But in both cases, there is still a clear focus toward the thing revealed or the thing presented as something separate, in a reality outside the poem. Williams needed the new painting to show him how the thing might be the work of art itself. Although he is not explicitly referring to Imagism yet, Williams's opposition to the implied separation between image and reality, or to the image as primarily *referential*, is already apparent in his censure in *Spring and All* of "the insignificant 'image' [which] may be 'evoked' never so ably and still mean nothing" (*Imaginations* 101). J. Hillis Miller, in his seminal early work on Williams's poetics, explains that the 1933 poem "The Locust Tree in Flower," for example, "is not a picture of the tree," but rather "an object which has the same kind of life as the tree," and which becomes "in itself something substantial [by] echoing in its structure of verbal forces the birth of white blossoms from stiff boughs" (304-05).

If we allow that, in the terms of Williams's late critique, Imagism's perceived lack of structure amounts to a lack of an equivalent "identity" between the structured object of the poem and the rest of reality, it might be worth concluding by focusing on the other structural relationship that his critique suggests is lacking in Imagism's tenets: namely, the implicit division between the poet, his poem, and the reality he intends for the latter to represent. "Do we think we stand outside the universe?" Williams asks rhetorically in the 1948 lecture cited above, in the discussion of structure and Imagism's want of it (*Selected Essays* 283). He even invokes a popular conception of Einstein to make his point here, using the metaphor of relativity to emphasize his own understanding of structure and reality: "Structure is where we come into contact with reality. And what is reality? How do we know reality? The only reality we can know is MEASURE" (*Selected Essays* 283). In the Cubist-Objectivist ideas outlined above, Williams proposes a kind of writing that would be *actual* in relation to the actuality of the rest of life "only to the extent that it would be pure design" (*Selected Essays* 98). Again though, as early as *Spring and All*, this "structural necessity" is matched with a sense that life itself "becomes actual only when it is identified with ourselves" (*Imaginations* 115). In other words, the echo of reality's structure in the material form of the poem-object is only substantiated by the perspective of a writing or reading subject, whose own measured and measuring existence is mutually affirmed by that dialectic.

Granted, it is a fairly abstract metaphysical point, but Williams is quite direct about the structurally interdependent "existence" of these three things: (1) the external object (whether a wheelbarrow or the whole universe), which only becomes actualized through our recognition— "when we name it, life exists" (*Imaginations* 115); (2) ourselves, who only exist by virtue of the language in which reader and poet are "locked in a fraternal embrace" (*Imaginations* 89); and (3) finally, of course, the poem itself—the poem that, with the structural paucity of Imagism's "free verse," of which Williams insists there is "no such thing," "had run down and become formally non extant" (*Autobiography* 264). It is, I contend, a rather extreme, if several times delayed, reaction to Imagism that ultimately serves as less a critique than a reiteration of principles arrived at in the meantime, which Imagism itself can hardly be blamed for lacking. In a 1958 essay on Zukofsky, Williams himself admits that "the intellectual meaning of the word [Imagism] was lost, we'll say, on me" (*Something to Say* 265). In this regard, Williams's critical remarks on Imagism might be better understood as using the earlier movement to signify his own immature period. Yet Williams's conception of structure and measure, which engender this "actualizing" correlation between self, object, and poem, does, I believe, articulate another revealing and legitimate response to the implied relationship between these three realms in the stated principles of Pound's Imagism.

## Notes

1. In a 1950 essay on "Mid-Century American Poets," Williams writes that "Pure Imagism is a dead mode," yet acknowledges its lesson "to quit filling in a set of dead lines with philosophic or other chatter and calling that a poem" (*Something to Say* 180).

2. In the interviews for *I Wanted To Write A Poem* (1958), when discussing his second book, *The Tempers*, which Pound had arranged to publish in London in 1913, Williams admits, "The poems of this period, short, lyrical, were more or less influenced by my meeting with Pound" (16); he also claims that in the early 1920s he was still throwing away good work because "I was afraid I was imitating Pound" (36).

3. The first two books of poetry are *Poems* (Rutherford, NJ: private printing, 1909) and *The Tempers* (London: Elkin Matthews, 1913).

4. Williams's complicated attitude toward Harriet Monroe is also evident in letters written at the same time as those to Lowell mentioned above (*Selected Letters* 38-39).

5. In one typical example, in the reprinting of *Spring and All* in *Imaginations* (1970), Webster Schott introduces the book thus: "In *Spring and All* [Williams] once and for all abandoned

the imagism and Keatsian classism [sic] of his three first books of poems" (*Imaginations* 86).

## Works Cited

Dijkstra, Bram. *The Hieroglyphics of New Speech: Cubism, Alfred Stieglitz and the Early Poetry of William Carlos Williams*. Princeton: Princeton UP, 1969. Print.

Kandinsky, Wassily. *Concerning the Spiritual in Art*. Trans. M. T. H. Sadler. New York: Dover, 1977. Print.

Kenner, Hugh. *The Pound Era*. Berkeley: U of California P, 1971. Print.

Mariani, Paul. *William Carlos Williams: A New World Naked*. New York: McGraw-Hill, 1981. Print.

Miller, J. Hillis. *Poets of Reality: Six Twentieth-Century Writers*. London: Oxford UP, 1966.

Pound, Ezra. *The Letters of Ezra Pound: 1907-1941*. Ed. D. D. Paige. New York: Harcourt, Brace, and World, 1950. Print.

---. "A Retrospect." *The Literary Essays of Ezra Pound*. Ed. T. S. Eliot. London: Faber & Faber, 1954. 3-14. Print.

Williams, William Carlos. *The Autobiography of William Carlos Williams*. New York: Random House, 1951. Print.

---. "The Basis of Poetic Form" (1941). Rpt. in *The Poker* 3 (2003): 22–29. Print.

---. *The Embodiment of Knowledge*. Ed. Ron Loewinsohn. New York: New Directions, 1974. Print.

---. *Imaginations*. Ed. Webster Schott. New York: New Directions, 1970. Print.

---. *I Wanted to Write a Poem: The Autobiography of the Works of a Poet*. Ed. Edith Heal. Boston: Beacon, 1958. Print.

---. *A Recognizable Image: William Carlos Williams on Art and Artists*. Ed. Bram Dijkstra. New York: New Directions, 1978. Print.

---. *The Selected Essays of William Carlos Williams*. New York: Random House, 1954. Print.

---. *The Selected Letters of Williams Carlos Williams*. Ed. John Thirlwall. New York: McDowell, Obolensky, 1957. Print.

---. *Something to Say: William Carlos Williams on Younger Poets*. Ed. James E. Breslin. New York: New Directions, 1985. Print.

Wilson, Guy, Dianne H. Pilgrim, and Dickran Tashjian. *The Machine Age in America: 1918-1941*. New York: Brooklyn Museum and Harry N. Abrams, 1986. Print.

# III. Imagism: Influence

# An Art of "Pure Sound Bound Through Symbols": Ezra Pound's Tutelage of Ernest Hemingway

Brad McDuffie

In the introduction to Ernest Hemingway's *Complete Poems*, Nicholas Gerogiannis states, "It would be a mistake to attribute much importance to [Hemingway's] poems in [his] artistic development" (xxi). Though it may be true that Hemingway never achieved the voice in his poetry that he did in prose, it seems that his early experiments with poetry were invaluable in laying the groundwork for his prose. As Wallace Stevens stated in 1942, "most people don't think of Hemingway as a poet, but obviously he is a poet and I should say, offhand, the most significant of living poets, so far as the subject of EXTRAORDINARY ACTUALITY is concerned" (qtd. in Gerogiannis xxiv). Accordingly, in his essay "Hemingway's Contribution to American Poetry," poet and critic Donald Junkins cites Ezra Pound's commanding influence upon Hemingway's formation as a writer: "Hemingway's early search for his vision led him directly to Pound, and it is no accident that Hemingway's fiction expresses itself within the guidelines that Pound advocated for poets" (18). The principles Hemingway learned from Pound can be traced throughout his fiction; however, it is the avant-garde novel *In Our Time* that best exemplifies Pound's Imagist sensibilities, especially through what Junkins terms the work's "juxtaposition of clarities" and "timing of economies" (19).

Indeed, T. S. Eliot's acknowledgment of Pound as *il miglior fabbro* of *The Waste Land* might just as well have been affixed to *In Our Time*. As K. K. Ruthven observes, "it is clear from Hemingway's testimony that Pound's procedure was to apply to fiction the critical methods he had designed a decade earlier in connection with *Imagiste* poetry" (125). In a 1925 letter, Hemingway requests that Pound review his *In Our Time* and tells him that "he had been the only person who had given him practical advice about prose" (qtd. in Tavernier-Courbin 181). In a later letter, Hemingway states that "he had learned more from Pound than from any other person" (qtd. in Tavernier-Courbin 181). It would appear that for *In Our Time* the *Imagiste* method has become law for Hemingway's prose. As H. R. Stoneback noted at the 2007 Imagism Conference at Brunnenburg Castle in Italy,

> Hemingway is the Imagist Poet that Pound called for in his critical writing in the decade before Hemingway's prose exploded on the Parisian scene. Go down the list—"direct treatment of the 'thing,'" no superfluous words, rhythm, no abstractions mixed with the concrete, the natural object as the adequate symbol, and so forth, and put an A+ next to Hemingway's name on every score. (131)

We might observe that *In Our Time* applies to prose the definition Pound gives to poetry in "I Gather the Limbs of Osiris": "It is an art of pure sound bound in through an art of arbitrary and conventional symbols. In so far as it is an art of pure sound, it is allied with music, painting, sculpture; in so far as it is an art of arbitrary symbols, it is allied to prose" (Pound, *Selected Prose* 33-34). Throughout *In Our Time*, Hemingway incorporates Pound's poetic language of "inspired mathematics" into the novel's "internal thought form" and "external symmetry" (qtd. in Singh 27, 29). Thus, *In Our Time* performs the essential function of Pound's art in that it frees prose from "the tyranny of the affects" (Singh 29) that he found abhorrent in the literature of the nineteenth century. Indebted to this vision, *In Our Time* made new the prose voice that would revolutionize the face of modern fiction.

According to M. L. Rosenthal, Pound "sought poetry in which sound, sense, and image must be functions of one another." These functions are founded upon traditional "models of organic composition" (7). Pound's "In

A Station of the Metro" illuminates that convergence of sound, sense, and image in that it creates what Pound termed a "radiant world in which one thought cuts through another with clean edge, a world of moving energies" (qtd. in Rosenthal 8). In this sense, the poem "presents an intellectual and emotional complex in an instant of time," though not one that uses "images as ornaments," but rather, as Wagner-Martin points out, as devices to "embody speed consistent with the moving eye, or moving mind, of the reader" (20). And Rosenthal adds, "In A Station of the Metro" creates "in miniature . . . the visualization of 'force in botanic terms,' the provision of 'borders' to define the 'shape' and 'loci' of contemporary experience" (9). With regards to the "shape" and "loci" of "contemporary experience," Hemingway distills Pound's *Imagiste* aesthetic throughout *In Our Time*. Pound's influence can be felt in the avant-garde shape of the composition itself, as well as in the book's intricately interwoven themes. Most notably, a close look at *In Our Time* can bring to light the manner in which Pound's influence penetrates to the very heart of the novel, from its overall framework to the minutiae. Indeed, Pound's DNA is evident even within the construction of Hemingway's sentences. Exploring Hemingway's use of structural super-positioning of sentences, images, and whole chapters in *In Our Time*, his poignant layering of images, and his impulse to "make it new" reveals how Pound's Imagist poetics shaped Hemingway's writing both stylistically and, in the end, thematically.

Applying Pound's conceptual principles of convergence to Hemingway's early drafts of *in our time*, as the work was originally entitled, is revelatory. The early version was made up entirely of vignettes that Hemingway would later use contrapuntally by alternating them with short stories in the second version, *In Our Time*. Hemingway wrote to Pound in 1923 commenting on revisions he has made, revisions Pound has seemingly advised:

> When they are read altogether they all hook up. It seems funny but they do. The bulls start, then reappear and then finish off. The war starts clear and noble just like it did . . . gets close and blurred and finished with the feller who goes home and gets clap. The refugees leave Thrace, due to the Greek ministers, who are shot. The whole thing closes with the King of Greece and his Queen in their Garden. . . . The last sentence is—Like all Greeks what he really wanted was to get to America. . . . The

radicals start noble in the young Magyar story and get bitched. America appears in the cops shooting the guys who robbed the cigar store. It has form all right. The king closes in swell shape. Oh that king. (*Selected Letters* 92)

It appears that Hemingway was intent on displaying both revisions and the overarching unity of the work to Pound. Furthermore, as John Peale Bishop writes, "In Paris, Hemingway submitted much of his apprentice work in fiction to Pound. It came back to him blue-penciled, most of the adjectives gone. The comments were unsparing. Writing for a newspaper was not at all the same as writing for a poet" (qtd. in Hurwitz 479). Hemingway's letter also captures Pound's poetic sensibility in that it speaks to both the moment in time and the movement of the image. Essentially, through the vignettes, Hemingway multiplies the *Imagiste* effect Pound distills in "In a Station of the Metro" by employing the principle of "placing image against image with no literal transition so that the reader's apprehension of meaning depends on his immediate response to the montage of concrete detail" (qtd. in Wagner-Martin 23). For example, in the story "Soldier's Home," Hemingway writes the following exchange between the soldier Krebs and his mother after Krebs returns home from the war and struggles to return to civilian life:

"I pray for you all day long, Harold." Krebs looked at the bacon fat hardening on his plate. (75)

The montage Hemingway creates by juxtaposing a prayer and bacon fat creates the same dynamic tension and instant of time that arises from Pound's juxtaposition, or super-positioning, of "apparitions" and "black bough" in "In A Station of the Metro."

As Stanley Coffman argues of Pound's super-positioning technique, "the images are so arranged that the pattern becomes an Image, an organic structure giving a force and pleasure that are greater than and different from the images alone" (qtd. in Witemeyer 35). To this Linda Wagner-Martin adds the effect of "organ base, Pound's notion that every piece of writing must have a controlling tone and shape appropriate to its basic meaning" (23). Thus, as Wagner-Martin concludes, it should not be surprising that Pound "described Hemingway as an 'imagist' in his fiction" (23).

When one sets "In a Station of a Metro" next to sentences from Hemingway's early *in our time* vignettes, Pound's influence can be simultaneously heard, sensed, and imaged.

Pound:

> The apparition of these faces in the crowd;
> Petals on a wet, black bough. (*Selected Poems* 35)

Then Hemingway:

> *They whack-whacked the white horse on the legs and he kneed himself up.* (*In Our Time* 89)

And

> *They hanged Sam Cardinella at six o-clock in the morning in the corridor of the county jail.* (143)

And

> *We sat down at a table under a big tree and the king ordered whiskey and soda.* (157)

Rosenthal's comments on "the visualization of force in botanic terms" and the "loci of contemporary experience" seem especially apt here. How appropriate that the "loci" of Hemingway's contemporary experience results in the paradox of the violent and the serene, which is also evident in Pound's "Station." The presence of the faces suspended in the sea of humanity boarding or unloading from the train corresponds with the omitted yet somehow looming presence of the Metro train in the station. "The notion of technological progress heaped lifestyle changes on the Western world more radical, perhaps, than written history ever recorded," Mary Karr writes, adding: "subways . . . whisked human beings through underground chasms in herds. . . . wholesale motorized murder was part and parcel of the increasingly mechanized world" (xii). Hemingway constantly reinforces the human conflict with the progress of the modern world in *In Our Time* by drawing attention to technologically disruptive and violent mechanisms, especially those associated with World War I, as he illuminates their effect upon characters both internally and externally, such as in the way he portrays a fragmented sense of place.

Another notable feature of Hemingway's letter to Pound is his explanation of his use of multiple symbols within the collection. For example, he identifies bullfighting and war as the two major themes of the early vignettes. As Harold M. Hurwitz relates in his essay "Hemingway's Tutor, Ezra Pound," Pound "recommended the use of an 'absolute rhythm which corresponds to the emotion or shade of emotion to be expressed.' Regarding symbols, he had remarked that 'the proper and perfect symbol is the natural object'" (477). By employing Pound's disciplined lesson from Flaubert of *le mot juste*, Hemingway had learned how to capture the musical quality of the symbol, and in the bullfight he found the perfect juxtaposition with the theme of war, as he conveyed in a letter to one of his fellow Red Cross ambulance drivers, William Horne: "It's a great tragedy . . . and takes more guts and skill and guts again than anything possibly could. It's just like having a ringside seat at the war with nothing going to happen to you" (*Selected Letters* 88).

In a letter to Edmund Wilson, Hemingway explains his use of counterpoint with the vignettes of *in our time* and the short stories of *In Our Time*. His description is in terms of sense and images that are disorienting "functions of one another" and "loci" (Rosenthal 9):

> Finished the book of 14 stories with a chapter . . . of [*in our time*] between each story—that is the way they were meant to go—to give the picture of the whole between examining it in detail. Like looking with your eyes at something, say a passing coast line, and then looking at it with 15X binoculars. Or rather, maybe, looking at it and then going in and living it—and then coming out and looking at it again. (*Selected Letters* 128)

It is evident through Hemingway's structural arrangement of shifting perspectives, as Wilson characterizes it, that *In Our Time* continues the thematic progression outlined in his letter to Pound. Furthermore, Hemingway fully realizes Pound's language of "inspired mathematics" through the work's "internal thought form" and "external symmetry." Notably, when Maxwell Perkins asked him to consider "rearranging the stories or grouping together all the vignettes" (Reynolds 49), Hemingway rejected the idea and told him firmly, "Max *please believe me* that those chapters are where they belong" (qtd. in Reynolds 49; Hemingway's emphasis). Perhaps the best example of the correspondence between form and content comes in "On the Quai at Smyrna," a type of "Introduction by the Author" (Reynolds 50) that Hemingway added to the 1930 edition of *In Our Time* at Perkins's request. With its opening line, "The strange thing was, he said, how they screamed every night at midnight" (*In Our Time* 12), "On the Quai at Smyrna" sets a tone that relates one of the central conflicts of the work: how the individual will cope with the chaos of the modern world in our time. This theme continues in the first chapter vignette when an adjutant tells the speaker, "*You must put it out. It is dangerous. It will be observed*" (13). The speaker, a "*kitchen corporal*," informs us, "*We were fifty kilometers from the front but the adjutant worried about the fire in my kitchen*" (13). Yet the psychological distance from the front for the speaker, who has not seen any conflict, is much greater than for the adjutant, who has. Here Hemingway shifts the external terror of war and women screaming at midnight to the shell-shocked adjutant worried that the caravan will be "observed" and draw fire from the enemy; this contrast itself, in other words, intensifies the trauma of the war's presence by underscoring its distance. In the next story, "Indian Camp," also set at night, Nick Adams's father, Dr. Adams, performs a Cesarean on a woman without "any anesthetic," and he tells Nick, "her screams are not important. I don't hear them because they are not important" (16), thereby echoing, yet re-contextualizing, the first line of "On the Quai at Smyrna." Though Hemingway provides no explanation or transition for the sequence of stories and vignettes, Nick's instruction, his rite-of-passage, in the story provides the central lens of experience within *In Our Time*.

By the final story, "Big Two-Hearted River," the terror and screams in the night converge when Nick returns home to try and recover from the internal and external wounds he has suffered during the war. As he makes his camp "in the good place" and finds his "home where he made it," his father's words from "Indian Camp"—about the need to focus on the important *life-saving* work beyond the screams—resonate with Nick's journey. "Big Two-Hearted River: Part I" begins with a "train" moving "out of sight" and Nick being left in a waste land of "burnt timber" and "burned-over country" (133). Hemingway carefully crafts the details in the scene to reflect the terror of the war and the effect it has had upon Nick: "Nick looked at the burned-over stretch of hillside, where he had expected to find the scattered houses of the town and then walked down the railroad track to the bridge over the river" (133). The super-positioning of the railroad tracks and the river—a juxtaposition of images that does not seem that far removed from the super-positioning of Pound's Metro station, apparitions, and black bough—conveys the intersection of the modern world and the natural world. Nick proceeds to look down at the trout "keeping themselves steady in the current with wavering fins" and "holding themselves with their noses into the current" as he watches them "in deep, fast moving water" (133). Hemingway's language throughout the opening of the story creates a series of objective correlatives between the country, Nick's decimated home land, and the trout, which represent Nick's need to hold himself steady as he recovers from the internal trauma the war has created in him. In the penultimate passage of the story's opening movement, Hemingway brings the central images of *In Our Time* together through an intense series of details in which the surface planes of Nick on the railroad bridge and the trout in river merge:

> Nick looked down into the pool from the bridge. It was a hot day. A kingfisher flew up the stream. It was a long time since Nick had looked into a stream and seen trout. They were very satisfactory. As the shadow of the kingfisher moved up the stream, a big trout shot upstream in a long angle, only his shadow marking the angle, then lost his shadow as he came through the surface of the water, caught the sun, and then, as he went back into the stream under the surface, his shadow seemed to float down the stream with the current, unresisting, to his post under the bridge where he tightened facing up into the current.
>
> Nick's heart tightened as the trout moved. He felt all the old feeling. (134)

In this passage, together with the imagery of the bridge and the trout in the stream, Hemingway adds a third plane of imagery with the "kingfisher." When Nick's heart "tightens," as the trout "tightened facing up into the stream," the "two hearts" of the story's title come together; and when the "shadow of the kingfisher moved up the stream" toward the bridge in tandem with the shadow of the trout, the allusion to Arthurian legend suggests that Nick also comes together with the Fisher King. Later in Part II, Nick moves into the water and Hemingway once again draws the two planes together —above and below the water—when he writes that Nick feels his "heart down" with the wounded trout in the water that is "holding himself steady over the gravel" (150). The image correlates with the young Nick Adams holding "his hand in the water" after a bass has "jumped, making a circle in the water," when he feels "quite sure that he would never die" (19). In this way, employing Imagist techniques, Hemingway charts the emotional trajectory of Nick Adams throughout *In Our Time*.

In addition to its use of juxtaposition, "Big Two-Hearted River" also seems to embody the still point of Imagism laid out by T. E. Hulme, who himself influenced Pound's doctrine of the image. Hulme characterizes Imagism as comprising "many diverse images by the convergence of their actions, direct consciousness to the precise point where there is a certain intuition to be seized" (qtd. in Hasbany 231). And Richard Hasbany adds that "it is the unity of a precise point when a reality, a truth is perceived that Hemingway is striving for. He tries to juxtapose thirty-two separate pieces, each a kind of image in itself, into a total image" (231). As Pound wrote, "Relations between things are more important than the things themselves" (qtd. in Karr xix). This dictum serves as a guide for navigating *In Our Time*, and it would seem that at the core of the "relations between things" in the book is the "total image" of the Fisher King: "Oh that king." Of course, Hemingway's invocation of the Fisher King recalls *The Waste Land*, and the influence of that poem upon Hemingway's avant-garde novel also culminates in "Big Two-Hearted River." The accretion of images outlined in Hemingway's 1923 letter to Pound seems to correspond precisely with Pound's own meditation on how a longer poem could operate in the modes of Imagism and Vorticism:

> I am often asked whether there can be a long imagiste or vorticist poem. The Japanese, who evolved the hokku, evolved also the Noh plays. In the best "Noh" the whole play may consist of one image. I mean it is gathered around one image. The unity consists in one image, enforced by movement and music. I see nothing against a long vorticist poem. (*Gaudier-Brzeska* 94)

"One image, enforced by movement and music," Pound writes, and this principle governs *In Our Time* throughout Nick's pilgrimage towards becoming a Fisher King. The effect of *In Our Time* can be compared to what William Pratt observes of "the later experiments in modern English poetry" in that "the longer poems of Williams, Pound, or Eliot" are "aggregate Imagist poems, set in a sort of mosaic pattern around a dominate image—a super-image, like *The Waste Land*" (53).

In the end, Hemingway and Pound found a common redemptive ground in the form of writing, which they both addressed with a type of priestly reverence. In the section Hemingway omits from "Big Two-Hearted River," later published as "On Writing," he gives what might be his greatest tribute to Pound: "Ezra thought fishing was a joke." The point here is that fishing and bullfighting render symbolic action that, when combined with the *deus loci*, creates the very action that Pound loved: writing. Nick tells us that writing, not fishing, "was really more fun than anything. That was really why you did it. He had never realized that before. . . . It had more bite to it than anything else" (*Nick Adams* 238). Then Nick meditates on Cézanne and states, "He wanted to write like Cezanne [*sic*] painted" (239), a passage reflective of Pound's statement that poetry is "an art allied . . . with painting" (*Selected Prose* 33). Pound's influence on Hemingway's prose resonates here, and Nick Adams seems to speak for him when he states: "he felt almost holy about it" (*Nick Adams* 239). The art of pure sound merges with the arbitrary symbol when Hemingway writes: "Nick, seeing how Cezanne [*sic*] would do the stretch of river and the swamp, stood up and stepped down into the stream . . . moving in the picture" (240), just as the speaker of Pound's "In a Station of the Metro," stepping into the metro station, might see how Monet would do the "faces in the crowd."

Pound's axiom to "make it new" offers life-giving potential to Hemingway and Nick Adams in the wake of World War I. Early in *In Our Time*, Nick learns "Nothing was ever lost" (48), even when it all seemed "so tragic" (49). The older Hemingway, it seems, echoes this same need to "make it new" when he remembers his loss in *A Moveable Feast*—"What did I know best that I had not written about and lost? What did I know about truly and care for the most?" (77)—and then meditates on loss, work, and the need to "make the country" (the waste land) new: "All I must do now was stay sound and good in my head until morning when I would start to work again" (77).

The most poignant example of rebuilding, remaking after loss, in *In Our Time* comes near the conclusion of Part I of "Big Two-Hearted River": "It had been a hard trip. He was very tired. That was done. He had made his camp. He was settled. Nothing could touch him. It was a good place to camp. He was there, in the good place. He was in his home where he had made it. Now he was hungry" (139). The word "made" appears twice in this passage and seems to draw us out of the text to note Hemingway, the writer, as the re-maker of "the good place." Hemingway's and Nick's remaking of the world is rooted in the past, also the central tenet of Pound's statement: to know the poets and traditions of the past and make them new. Here, Hemingway invokes the creation account in the book of Genesis: "And God called the dry land Earth and the gathering together of the waters called the Seas: and God saw that it was good" (1.10). The "good" of creation, of making it new, also echoes the existential philosophy of Ecclesiastes, Hemingway's favorite book of the Bible: "There is nothing better for a man, than that he should eat and drink, and that he should make his soul enjoy good in his labor" (2.24).

Early on in *A Moveable Feast*, Hemingway writes that he was "learning something from the painting of Cézanne that made writing simple true sentences far from enough to make the stories have the dimensions that I was trying to put in them. I was learning very much from him but I was not articulate enough to explain it to anyone. Besides it was a secret" (13). Years later Hemingway confided to his wife Mary that "nobody really knows or understands and nobody has ever said the secret. The secret is that it is poetry written into prose and it is the hardest of all things to do" (Mary Hemingway, *How It Was* 305). To understand Hemingway's secret, it is clear that one must understand what he learned from "his most important writing mentor," who both knew the secret of writing poetry into prose and generously shared it: Ezra Pound. And only by understanding Pound's early tutelage of Hemingway can we understand the modernist, imagist, and vorticist sensibilities that grounded him as a young writer and resonated in his writing for the rest of his life.

## Works Cited

Gerogiannis, Nicholas. "Introduction." *Complete Poems*. By Ernest
    Hemingway. Lincoln: U of Nebraska P, 1992. xi-xxviii. Print.
*The Holy Bible*. King James Version. Nashville: Holman, 1982. Print.
Hasbany, Richard. "The Shock of Vision: An Imagist Reading of In Our
    Time." *Ernest Hemingway: Five Decades of Criticism*. Ed. Linda Wagner-
    Martin. East Lansing: Michigan State UP, 1974. 224-40. Print.
Hemingway, Ernest. *In Our Time*. New York: Scribner, 1996. Print.
---. *A Moveable Feast*. New York: Scribner, 1964. Print.
---. *The Nick Adams Stories*. New York: Scribner, 2003. Print.
---. *Selected Letters 1916-1961*. Ed. Carlos Baker. New York: Scribner,
    1981. Print.
Hemingway, Mary. *How It Was*. New York: Knopf, 1976. Print.
Hurwitz, Harold M. "Hemingway's Tutor, Ezra Pound." *Modern Fiction
    Studies* 17 (1971-72): 469-82. Print.
Junkins, Donald. "Hemingway's Contribution to American Poetry."
    *Hemingway Review* 4.2 (1985): 18-23. Print.
Karr, Mary. "How to Read *The Waste Land* So It Alters Your Soul Rather
    Than Just Addling Your Head." Introduction. *The Waste Land and Other
    Writings*. By T. S. Eliot. New York: Modern Library, 2001. ix-xxviii.
    Print.
Kenner, Hugh. *The Pound Era*. Berkeley: U of California P, 1971. Print.
Pound, Ezra. *Gaudier-Brzeska*. New York: New Directions, 1970. Print.
---. *Selected Poems of Ezra Pound*. New York: New Directions, 1957. Print.
---. *Selected Prose 1909-1965*. New York: New Directions, 1973. Print.
Pratt, William. *The Imagist Poem: Modern Poetry in Miniature*. 3rd ed. New
    Orleans: U of New Orleans P, 2008. Print.
Reynolds, Michael. *Hemingway: the 1930s*. New York: W. W. Norton, 1997.
    Print.
Rosenthal, M. L. *A Primer of Ezra Pound*. New York: Macmillan, 1960.
    Print.
Ruthven, K. K. *Ezra Pound as Literary Critic*. New York: Routledge, 1990.
    Print.
Singh, G. *Ezra Pound as Critic*. New York: St. Martin's, 1994. Print.
Stoneback, H. R. "'Only Emotion Endures'–No 'Emotional Slither': or
    Hemingway and Imagism." *Florida English* 6 (2008): 129-32. Print.
Tavernier-Courbin, Jacqueline. "Ernest Hemingway and Ezra Pound."
    *Ernest Hemingway: The Writer in Context*. Ed. James Nagel. Madison: U
    of Wisconsin P, 1984. 179-200. Print.
Wagner-Martin, Linda W. *Hemingway and Faulkner: Inventors/Masters*.
    Metuchen, NJ: Scarecrow P, 1975. Print.
Witemeyer, Hugh. *The Poetry of Ezra Pound: Forms and Renewal, 1908-
    1920*. Berkeley: U California P, 1969. Print.

# "A Few Don'ts" in *The Torrents of Spring*

Roy Verspoor

In "A Retrospect" Ezra Pound writes: "It is better to present one Image in a lifetime than to produce voluminous works" (18). Looking at Hemingway's works, we find a collection of images that are repeated throughout. These images were with Hemingway from the beginning and remained as touchstones throughout his career. In "The Big Two-Hearted River," Hemingway writes: "Nick's heart tightened as the trout moved. He felt all the old feeling" (164). The image of a trout moving occurs elsewhere in "The End of Something" (80), "The Undefeated" (196), and again in Chapter XII of *The Sun Also Rises* (119). Similarly, we can look at the repeated image of water moving against the piles of bridges, or the repeated use of the pillar image alone. Readers will remember how often protagonists remain silent after a flawed character speaks, or the recurring image of bread being used to mop up the last juice of a meal. From his earliest work in *In Our Time*, Hemingway was dedicated to finding the perfect image, the image that would present the emotional core of the scene intuitively, rather than explicitly.

This artistic goal and the way in which these presentations are crafted have become indicative of Hemingway's style, but they are also related to the goals and guidelines of Imagism, as proposed by Ezra Pound. The actuality and clarity of Hemingway's earliest prose gains its strength from its direct treatment of character and landscape, its economy with language, and the rhythm of its sentences. Some of the most characteristic aspects of Hemingway's style are essentially major principles of the Imagist movement. These artistic similarities become noticeable in his earliest fiction by observing how emotion is created in these stories. Hemingway's commitment to imagistic principles can also be seen in his parody of bad writing, where he playfully violates these principles. The prime example of this parody is *The Torrents of Spring*, Hemingway's purposely horrendous book, which was scrawled in only ten days. Hemingway's publisher, Horace Liveright, would not accept the novel; its satire and lampooning made it a "cold-blooded contract-breaker" (Baker 160). Liveright could not rightly publish the book because he thought its parody "made a bum" of Sherwood Anderson (Baker 162), who in the winter of 1925 was Liveright's best selling author. By rejecting the book, Liveright freed Hemingway from his (unwanted) contract, and Hemingway was then able to sign with Max Perkins at Scribners, where he remained for his career. Though widely considered negligible, *The Torrents of Spring* remains in print and can be a useful resource for writers, providing instructional value similar to Pound's "A Few Don'ts" as a guide for how *not* to write. Pound's influence on *Torrents* is likely, considering the time and place of its composition. Hemingway was then solidifying his views as a writer, and Ezra Pound was always eager to dispense his advice.

The friendship of Pound and Hemingway is no mystery, and Pound's value as a mentor is easy to trace. If Hemingway may be considered an apprentice of Pound at anytime, it would be during his Paris years as he penned his earliest fiction. Later in life Hemingway praised Pound as "the most generous writer I have ever known. . . . He helped poets, painters, sculptors and prose writers that he believed in and he would help anyone whether he believed in them or not if they were in trouble" (*A Moveable Feast* 115-16). This generosity extended to Hemingway. In 1922 Pound asked Hemingway to contribute his work to a collection that would act as "an inquest into the state of contemporary English," to be published by William Bird and Three Mountain Press (qtd. in Baker 100). In a conversation with Ford Madox Ford, Pound praised Hemingway further: "He's an experienced journalist. He writes very good verse and he's the finest prose stylist in the world. . . . He's disciplined too" (qtd. in Baker 123). Later, when asked to submit a tribute for Pound, Hemingway would write: "any poet born in this century or in the last ten years of the preceding century who can honestly say that he has not been influenced by or learned greatly from the work of Ezra Pound deserves to be pitied rather than rebuked. . . . The best of Pound's writing . . . will last as long as there is any literature" (qtd. in Baker 236). Even later, in *A Moveable Feast*, Hemingway would comment, "[Ezra's] own writing, when he would hit it right, was so perfect, and he was so sincere in his mistakes and so enamored of his errors, and so kind to people that I always thought of him as a sort of saint" (114).

This mutual admiration is evident throughout each writer's nonfiction and letters, but what is more valuable is tracing Pound's artistic influence within Hemingway's actual writing. In 1912, over tea in Kensington, Pound, along with H.D. and Richard Aldington, agreed upon three criteria for good poetry: to treat the "thing" directly, to use no unnecessary word, and to compose in the sequence of a musical phrase. Considering his relationship with Pound during those early Parisian years, it would be farfetched to think that Hemingway was unfamiliar with these teachings. Later in his life he would praise these aspects of Pound's poetry and his role as a teacher. In 1922, he wrote, "[Ezra is] teaching me to write and I'm teaching him to box" (qtd. in Baker 86). In *A Moveable Feast*, Hemingway writes, Pound was "the man I liked and trusted the most as a critic then, the man who believed in the mot juste—the one and only correct word to use—the man who had taught me to distrust adjectives as I would later learn to distrust certain people in certain situations" (136).

In his valuable essay "Hemingway's Tutor, Ezra Pound," Harold Hurwitz describes Hemingway's use of economy in the editing process. Between the first and last drafts of the *In Our Time* vignette that begins "*Minarets stuck up in the rain*," "Hemingway reduced the 241 words to 121, the more than thirty descriptive adjectives to ten, and made every one of them hard and clear" (14). This precise and disciplined craftsmanship and its impact on Hemingway's earliest fiction were well-noted in the *New York Times Book Review* of *In Our Time*, in which the unnamed reviewer acclaimed Hemingway's language as "hard and clear" and noted that his "prose seems to have an organic being of its own." Furthermore, the critic writes that the prose exerts "an authentic energy and propulsive force which is contained in an almost primitive isolation of images, as if the language itself were being made over in its early directness of metaphor. Each story, indeed, is a sort of expanded metaphor, conveying a far larger implication than its literal meaning" (qtd. in Hasbany 229).

The reviewer skates around describing a technique we may recognize as fundamentally Imagist. The ultimate end of both Imagism and Hemingway's fiction begs the reader to respond intuitively to a text, rather than intellectually. This is the purpose of the objective correlative, "a concept based ultimately in the ideas of the imagist" (Hasbany 226), as well as of Hemingway's theory of omission. In describing the flagship poem of the Imagist movement, "In the Station of the Metro," Pound explains: "In a poem of this sort one is trying to record the precise instant when a thing outward and objective transforms itself, or darts into a thing inward and subjective" (*Gaudier-Brzeska* 89). The goal of Imagism is to capture for the reader the image that causes the emotion, or in Hemingway's words, to capture that "which produced the emotion that you experienced . . . the real thing the sequence of motion and fact which made the emotion" (*Death in the Afternoon* 2). To reach this goal the writer must follow the advice given by Nick Adams in "On Writing": "You could do it if you would fight it out. If you'd lived right with your eyes" (*Ernest Hemingway on Writing* 239). The writer must know what to include and what to omit. His language and observations must be exact. His cadence must be natural, not forced. These techniques allow for the presentation of "an intellectual and emotional complex in an instant of time" and for the "sense of sudden liberation; that sense of freedom from time limits and space limits; that sense of sudden growth" (Pound, "A Retrospect" 18). They also allow the audience to "feel more than they understand" (Hemingway, *A Moveable Feast* 75). When asked "How can a writer train himself?" Hemingway once responded: "Watch what happens today. If we get into a fish see exactly what it is that everyone does. If you get a kick out of it while he is jumping remember back until you see exactly what the action was that gave you the emotion" (*Ernest Hemingway On Writing* 30). The advice here is to find the catalyst that causes the emotion, essentially to find the image of the moment.

Hemingway reached this goal by following the proposed techniques of Imagism, by being as direct as possible with description and by tightening his prose. Imagistic technique can also be seen through what Pound and Hemingway reject. In "A Retrospect" (1918) Pound explains the goals of Imagism negatively through a list of "A Few Don'ts." The list includes such bits of advice as "Use no superfluous word, no adjective which does not reveal something"; "Don't use such an expression as 'dim lands of peace.' . . .

It mixes an abstraction with the concrete"; "Use either no ornament or good ornament"; "Don't be descriptive"; and "Don't make each line stop dead at the end, and then begin every next line with a heave" ("A Retrospect" 4-7). Likewise, Hemingway points to the principles of his craft through negative example in his satire *The Torrents of Spring*. Just as Hemingway's good fiction works in concordance with Imagism's "three propositions," his satire acts as an example of what happens when the Imagist advice is ignored.

In this short novella, Hemingway *does* just about all of Pound's "Don'ts." The humor of the book comes from his inept diction and style. One of the main characters of *Torrents of Spring*, Scripps, is a writer whose technique is in sharp contrast with Hemingway's own as well as with the principles of Imagism. Scripps's thoughts treat nothing directly. He is vague and forgetful, stumbling over quotations and second-guessing himself again and again. The narrator also shares this aloofness and complete inaccuracy of treatment. For example, he describes the second major character, Yogi Johnson, as "a chunky, well-built fellow. One of the sort you see around almost anywhere. He looked as though he had been through things" (28). The characterization is done so poorly that little actual imagery and no distinctive emotion could ever be drawn out. There are also moments that are so vague as to be contradictory: "In some ways it was the happiest year of his life. In other ways it was a nightmare. A hideous nightmare. In the end he grew to like it. In other ways he hated it" (31). The descriptions of setting are equally imprecise. In Brown's Beanery, "There was a long counter. There was a clock. There was a door led into the kitchen. There were a couple tables. There were a pile of doughnuts under a glass cover. There were signs put about on the wall advertising things one might eat" (17). The description is generic, lacking any distinctive detail to set the Beanery apart from any other restaurant, and it reads "in the sequence of" a metronome, not a "musical phrase," with the repetition of "there was/ were" at the start of each similarly constructed sentence. Compare the difference in effect with the café description from *The Sun Also Rises*: "I saw the long zinc bar. Outside on the terrace working people were drinking. In the open kitchen of the Amateurs a girl was cooking potato-chips in oil. There was an iron pot of stew. The girl ladled some onto a plate for an old man who stood holding a bottle of red wine in one hand" (77). Here precise observation and rhythmic variety conjure up a vivid scene.

Along with its indirect treatment of people and places, *The Torrents of Spring* is verbose in the extreme. It is clear that Hemingway is overloading his lines for comic effect, either with unnecessary adverbs, as in "He shook his head ruefully and smiled at the men, a little grimly perhaps" (5), or needless repetition: "They looked at him, but their faces did not change. Their faces remained the same" (14). Scripps realizes an economy of language could help his writing, but even this realization is loaded with superfluous words:

> He would cut the story short. He would give the bare essentials. Besides, it was beastly cold. It was cold standing there on the wind-swept station platform. Something told him it was useless to go on. He looked over at the deer lying there in a pile, stiff and cold. Perhaps they, too, had been lovers. Some were bucks and some were does. The bucks had horns. That was how you could tell. With cats it is more difficult. In France they geld the cats and do not geld the horses. France was a long way off. (14)

These lines provide everything but the bare essentials. The weather is described outright more than once, but no concrete detail follows to draw the reader into the scene. Instead, readers are treated to the meandering of Scripps's thoughts, full of trivial facts and pointless imaginings that begin and end nowhere.

It may already be clear that *Torrents* also goes against the last major principle of Imagism—to compose in a musical phrase—but this fault is made explicit in the description of Scripps: "Drinking robbed him of his ear for music. Times when he was drunk the sound of the whistles of the trains at night pulling up the Boyne Falls grade seemed more lovely than anything this chap Stravinsky had ever written" (7). His ignorance about music is noticeable in almost every line. Readers cannot help but stumble over a line such as "The single moment of spiritual communion they had had, had been dissipated. They had never really had it. But they might have" (14); or this choppy string of fragmented thoughts, "The girl was trying to take him away. Him, her Scripps. Trying to take him away. Take him away. Could she, Diana, hold him?" (42). Hemingway's later prose is appreciated for its poetic qualities; the knobby, brambly language of *Torrents* gains its humor by demonstrating the qualities that Pound and

Imagism would reject.

While many found *Torrents* to be too controversial and unnecessarily harsh with its criticism of writers like Sherwood Anderson, Pound thought it was well done. He wrote to Hemingway: "The only disserptmnt I had re/ Torrents wuz that you didn't land a few more bots to the Jaw" (*Letters* 230). Pound would have no reason to dislike the satire; it criticized a style that he also found faulty, a style that makes it impossible for a successful image to be translated and for a sincere emotion to be found. Hemingway's parody shows how useful the propositions of Imagism can be by illustrating how disastrous fiction can become when they are ignored. The effort here is not to prove that Hemingway was a covert Imagist, nor to affirm that Pound was a superior Imagist, but rather to acknowledge the importance of Pound's Imagist advice in regard to craft. The three propositions set forth by Pound are instructive not only for would-be Imagists, but for all writers.

## Works Cited

Baker, Carlos. *Ernest Hemingway: A Life Story*. New York: Scribner, 1969. Print.

Hasbany, Richard. "The Shock of Vision: An Imagist Reading of In Our Time." *Ernest Hemingway: Five Decades of Criticism*. Ed. Linda W. Wagner. Ann Arbor: Michigan State UP, 1974. 224-40. Print.

Hemingway, Ernest. *Death in the Afternoon*. New York: Scribner 1932. Print.

---. *Ernest Hemingway on Writing*. Ed. Larry W. Phillips. New York: Scribner, 1984. Print.

---. *A Moveable Feast*. New York: Scribner, 1964. Print.

---. *The Sun Also Rises*. New York: Scribner, 2006. Print.

---. *The Torrents of Spring*. New York: Scribner, 2004. Print.

Hurwitz, Harold M. "Hemingway's Tutor, Ezra Pound." *Ernest Hemingway: Five Decades of Criticism*. Ed. Linda W. Wagner. Ann Arbor: Michigan State UP, 1974. 8-21. Print.

Pound, Ezra. *Letters, 1907-1941*. Ed. D. D. Paige. New York: Harcourt, 1950. Print.

---. *Gaudier-Brzeska*. New York: New Directions, 1970. Print.

---. "A Retrospect." *Literary Essays of Ezra Pound*. Ed. T. S Eliot. New York: New Directions, 1954. 3-15. Print.

# James Laughlin: Unacknowledged Imagist

Ian S. MacNiven

When a person's poetic lineage begins with Ezra Pound and William Carlos Williams, and that person goes on to produce a *Collected Poems 1935-1997*, in process at this moment, that will run to 1,200 pages, it should come as no surprise that many traces of the Imagism in verse practiced early on by both Pound and Williams will appear in the work of their acolyte. So it is with James Laughlin, who met Pound in 1933 and Williams two years later. Best known as the founder of the New Directions Publishing Corporation, Laughlin combined his press business with developing the Alta ski area outside Salt Lake City, and he took time out for five years to run Intercultural Publications for the Ford Foundation in the 1950s. But his first and his last love was poetry, and during his long life Laughlin completed over a score of volumes of poetry, counting as the greatest honor ever bestowed upon him his induction as a *poet* into the American Academy of Arts and Letters. His own reputation as a poet was overshadowed by his renown as the publisher of other poets—including Robert Creeley, Robert Duncan, Lawrence Ferlinghetti, Federico García Lorca, H.D., Denise Levertov, Thomas Merton, Pablo Neruda, Kenneth Patchen, Octavio Paz, Kenneth Rexroth, Gary Snyder, Dylan Thomas—and by his modest reluctance to send out his own books to reviewers. Laughlin should eventually come to be widely recognized as a fine poet, and his first flowering in verse came under the influence of two of the first proclaimed Imagists.

The origins of the Imagist movement are well known. The English philosopher T. E. Hulme was in Brussels teaching English and reading Henri Bergson in 1907, and this led him to Paris and a meeting with Bergson. Then Hulme returned to London, where he established The Poets' Club to promote the ideas about the image in poetry that he had derived from his discussions with Bergson. Hulme wrote five exemplary poems to illustrate what he called "Imagism," published in 1911 in the journal *New Age* under the tongue-in-cheek title, "The Complete Poetical Works of T. E. Hulme." It remained for Richard Aldington, H.D., and Pound in 1912 to write a few poems following Hulme's pattern, and then in discussion the trio formulated the tenets of Imagist writing, based on Hulme: "(1) direct treatment of the subject; (2) to allow no word that was not essential to the presentation, and (3) in their rhythms to follow the musical phrase rather than strict regularity" (Stock 115). To simplify further, Imagism meant for them *directness, economy, musical phrasing*. Then Pound, an inveterate editor, compiled *Des Imagistes*, the first Imagist anthology, in 1912, a volume that included the three Imagist standard-bearers, together with Williams, D. H. Lawrence, Amy Lowell, and five other poets. Lowell leapt in to edit three more Imagist anthologies, which Pound, never happy marching to someone else's beat, dubbed "Amygism," and to which he did *not* contribute.

After a brief meeting with Pound in 1933, Laughlin took a leave-of-absence from Harvard and arrived at Pound's informal Ezuversity in Rapallo, Italy, in November 1934. According to Laughlin's own account, "The Boss," as he called Pound, refused to look at his prose but would occasionally critique his attempts at verse, stabbing and slashing with a blunt pencil, crossing out superfluous words and lines, and occasionally adding a few of his own. Although Laughlin would invariably claim in later years that Pound had told him bluntly to abandon poetry, as I have argued previously, this was probably not what he said and certainly not what Laughlin did: in the months and years following Laughlin's two relatively short sojourns at the Ezuversity, he would continue to send poems to The Boss, and Pound would at times give his imprimatur: "Let it be published." What does seem to be the case is that Pound was not a *deliberate* formative influence on Laughlin's poetry: that is, he did not attempt to mold his pupil's prosodic method. Rather, Pound gave him the sort of general advice he gave to everyone in writing, from James Jesus Angleton (future Director of Counterintelligence at the CIA) to Louis Zukofsky, Objectivist poet: to Make It New, cut out deadwood, follow the music of the inner ear, not the metronome. Also, soon to become Pound's American publisher, Laughlin discovered that The Boss set great store by the way words, spacings, and lines appeared on the page.

The Cantos may seem rife with allusion—and they are—but for Pound the many allusions are not intended as a reference back to some distant past, but to an associative present in the context of the poem. When Pound in St. Elizabeths asylum places Apollonius of Tyana in Canto 91, his presence is not historical, is not *then* but *now*, part of the world of *The Cantos*, sharing reality and contemporaneity with the mythical Merlin, the historical Francis Drake, and the incarcerated poet himself, who cries out, "I wd / like to see Verona again" (634). Laughlin too set out to make the classics and his own life part of the present tense of his poems. This had been a precept of the first great teacher in young Laughlin's life, the poet and classicist translator Dudley Fitts, and a precept followed with a kind of holy intensity by such proto-Imagists as H.D. and Aldington.

As Pound charged off in his own particular direction, multi-lingual, allusive, world-focused rather than stubbornly regional American, Bill Williams remained close to the tenets of Imagism, encapsulating as a ground rule for his own poetry, "No ideas / but in things" (*Collected Poems*). To this, at least, Pound—and Laughlin—remained in agreement. Williams called for the "thingness" of poetry. Pound insisted, "Any tendency to abstract general statement is a greased slide" (qtd. in Creeley 5).

Laughlin's pre-Ezuversity verse is derivative and often has an antique ring, an echo of Nordic twilight. One of these, "Sleep," with as an epigraph four lines from Macbeth's "ravel'd sleave of care" monologue, contains this stanza:

> Who waits in vain for sleep will know the pain
> Parched land must feel waiting for the rain.
> In sleep we journey far, sailing strange seas,
> Hearing new tongues, crossing eternities.
> Sleeping we are ourselves, stripped of all pride;
> Sleeping the heart and soul walk side by side.

It is a self-conscious and earnest stanza, opening with a line in iambic pentameter, the meter varied in the subsequent lines, but hobbled by regular rhymes. Not that the young poet had not been exposed to other forms: Dudley Fitts had assigned Cummings, Eliot, Pound, Stein, and Williams to his pupils in honors English at Choate. However, before Pound's stabbing pencil, Laughlin was trying to learn by imitation, and he wrote a quantity of such verse.

"A Birthday Fugue," probably drafted soon after Laughlin had enrolled at the Ezuversity, scans like an homage to Mr. lower-case cummings of No. 4 Patchin Place:

> hot sea calm
> and mind whirl
> these hours of words
>
> mind whirl
> o troubled land
> be gentle
>
> hot sea calm
> words turning
> turn to you
>
> these hours
> i give you
> o gentle
>
> sea. . . . (*Collected Poems* 3)

Most lines are only two or three syllables; the language is pared to bare bones; the image of the calm sea is repeated, economically; the words *whirl*, *troubled*, and *turning* imply rather than proclaim a mind not at rest; the rhythm calls to mind incantation, musical phrasing rather than a conventional metric pattern. It is, I submit, an Imagist poem.

Very soon after meeting Pound and Williams, Laughlin developed what he called his "typewriter metric," which he was careful to define as a format in which the first line set the line standard for the entire poem: each line was to vary no more than plus or minus two letters in length from the first line.

Spaces counted the same as letters. In Laughlin's mind, this regularity gave him a structure, just as Pound's far more arbitrary line lengths and spacings defined the appearance of his verse on a page. Laughlin had Pound's implied sanction: "verse usually has some element roughly fixed and some other that varies," Pound had written, "but which element is to be fixed and which vary . . . is the affair of the author" (*ABC* 201). Laughlin's inspiration for the name of his verse form had, however, come from Williams, a great one for metrical theory, who called his own "triadic line" "the variable foot." Williams told him early on that "the typewriter was the vehicle of the new age, and that I'd better use it" (Laughlin, "Interview"). Laughlin would write late in his life, "The point of the screwball metric," strictly limiting variation in line length, "is that the visual pattern of the couplets works against the sound of the underlying cadences which are from plain speech" (Letter to Dr. D. Romanos). In adopting this visual regularity, Laughlin did not, however, discard the directness, the economy of diction, or the musical phrasing of the Imagists.

Laughlin would employ his typewriter metric frequently for the rest of his life. An early example of it is found in "What My Head Did to Me"—which he insisted be printed in the Courier font of his typewriter, retaining the spacing of his typing. In this poem Laughlin eschews poetic diction; the language is direct and concrete. The "head" he refers to is a bust of him, sculpted by Lilian Swann, a young woman he was enamored of—but she married the architect Eero Saarinen instead. I have identified Swann because there is emotional baggage behind the poet's bland mention in the poem of the "woman" artist:

```
I guess I like myself
pretty well anyway I
wanted a statue of my-
self so I had a woman

make one it was a head
and she modelled it in
clay then one night I
dreamed I'd killed my

very best friend and
```

```
there was my head right
there ready to tell on
me when the police came

I tried to destroy the
face so they wouldn't
know it was me but my
hands stuck tight in

the clay I couldn't
tear them loose and
there I was when the
police came held by my

own head with the body
of my friend multi-
plying itself like
endless mirrors down

the street that's the
thing my head did to
me but of course it
was only a dream see.
```

(*Collected Poems* 7)

The persona of the narrator speaks in a voice Laughlin used fairly often: a self-satisfied conceit undercut by the speaker's distress, a distress that seems real even though he tries to pass it off lightly in the final lines, "but of course it / was only a dream see." The title too is loaded, and "the / thing my head did to / me" hints at mental imbalance. By the time Laughlin wrote this poem, his father had been institutionalized several times for severe bipolar breakdowns, and his grandfather had spent the last years of his life closely guarded by male keepers at his Florida mansion. Various uncles had suffered from the same malady. Throughout his life, Laughlin would worry about what his own head might do to him.

By 1936 Laughlin had founded New Directions and had published both

Pound and Williams. The story of Williams and New Directions would be
the saga of the evolution and publishing of *Paterson*, much as the story of
Pound and the publishing house would revolve around his *Cantos*. *Paterson*
stood for Williams himself: "That is why I started to write *Paterson*: a
man is indeed a city," he acknowledged. What a poet needed were things,
details, that he knew intimately, "an image large enough to embody the
whole knowable world about me" (*Autobiography* 390). Laughlin often
said that Pound and Williams were the twin polar axes of New Directions,
and that Pound was his "spiritual father," yet he also made it clear that he
considered Williams his mentor *in poetry*. Pound kept hammering away
at Williams—and at Laughlin—with the dictum that a poem must *mean*,
must have a "MESSAGE!" "You ask ol' Ez, he'll tell you," mocked Williams,
who just as stubbornly maintained the supremacy of the *thing* (Witemeyer
61): a "thinker" uses "'thought' as the net to put his thoughts into," but if
he leaves out the thing, "in the particular to discover the universal," he
will write a bad poem, one "to make a pigeon roar" (*Autobiography* 391).
Williams readily acknowledged Pound's wonderful ear for the sound
and weight of syllables, the melody line and brick-and-mortar of poetry.
Laughlin listened attentively to both his elders: Pound for sound, Williams
for image.

And there was a third elder in Laughlin's poetic ancestry: Eliot. When
Laughlin commended to Williams Eliot's *The Family Reunion*, he must have
known he was in for trouble: "if you want to see poetry as is poetry—hard
as a rock and beautiful as the queen's tit—look at the choruses in Eliot's new
play," he wrote to Williams (Witemeyer 43n). "I'm glad you like his verse,"
Williams fired back by return mail, "but I'm warning you, the only reason
it doesn't smell is that it's synthetic. . . . Birdseye Foods, suddenly frozen at
50 degrees below zero" (Witemeyer 40-41). Williams granted Eliot's ability
*as a writer*, but he blamed Eliot and Pound—"Pound less than Eliot"—for
wanting to dictate to the artist: "They want to *tell* him, right enough but
not to serve him" (Witemeyer 44). It was the old quarrel between tradition
and "something hot from the blood that, at its best, uses the traditional
literary and makes the great masterpieces of the world" (Witemeyer 43).
Williams spoke with all the passionate intensity of his mother's Puerto
Rican Latinity, and, although Laughlin conceded nothing, finally he owed
allegiance to Williams. When Williams praised two of Laughlin's poems,
one of them being "Easter in Pittsburgh," he was "mightily cheered." To

Williams, he explained that he sought to "get an effect of tension from the war between the strictly artificial visual pattern and the strictly natural spoken rhythms." This was not what Williams, Pound, *or* Eliot was doing, but Laughlin could trace elements of his own prosodic practice to all three of his elders: Williams for simplicity of statement and commonplace imagery; Pound for linguistic inventiveness and European allusions; the Eliot of the plays for the natural rhythms of conversation. Laughlin aimed, he said, to "try to write concretely, using everyday objects for your symbols and allegories, and to avoid poeticisms" (Witemeyer 45-46).

A decade after leaving the Ezuversity, Laughlin published a self-deprecatory version of an "Ars Poetica" (in the original his long-time friend Archibald MacLeish had written, "A poem should be wordless / As the flight of birds"). His own poem Laughlin entitled "What the Pencil Writes":

```
Often when I go out I
put in my coat pocket

some paper and a pen-
cil in case I want to

write something down
well there they are

wherever I go and as
my coat moves the pen-

cil writes by itself
a kind of gibberish

hieroglyphic which I
often think as I un-

dress at night & take
out those papers with

nothing written on
them but strange and
```

```
meaningless marks is
the story of my life.
```
*(Some Natural Things* 45)

Wordless marks like the footprints of birds. So Laughlin set about forging a style: concrete image patterns after Williams; innovation and *message* after Pound; conversational speech patterns echoing Eliot, Pound, and Williams; and Laughlin's own odd but simple typewriter metric. It added up to Imagism with his personal twist.

## Works Cited

Creeley, Robert. Introduction. *Charles Olson, Selected Writings.* By Charles Olson. New York: New Directions, 1996. Print.

Laughlin, James. *The Collected Poems 1935-1997.* New York: New Directions, 2012. Print.

---. Interview by Charlie Rossiter. "Introducing James Laughlin." New York State Council of the Arts. 1996. Web.

---. Letter to Dr. D. Romanos. 25 Dec. 1991. TS. Laughlin Papers. Meadow House, Norfolk, CT.

---. "Sleep." May 1934? TS. Laughlin Papers. Meadow House, Norfolk, CT.

---. *Some Natural Things.* Norfolk, CT: New Directions, 1945. Print.

MacLeish, Archibald. *The Collected Poems 1917-1952.* Boston: Houghton Mifflin, 1952. Print.

Pound, Ezra. *ABC of Reading.* 1934. New York: New Directions, 1960. Print.

---. *The Cantos of Ezra Pound.* New York: New Directions, 1996. Print.

Stock, Noel. *The Life of Ezra Pound: An Expanded Edition.* San Francisco: North Point Press, 1982. Print.

Williams, William Carlos. *Autobiography.* New York: Random House, 1951.

---. *The Collected Poems 1939-1962.* Vol. 2. Ed. Christopher MacGowan. New York: New Directions, 1988. Print.

Witemeyer, Hugh, ed. *William Carlos Williams and James Laughlin: Selected Letters.* New York: Norton, 1989. Print.

# Afterword

# On Imagism & Hymnagism:
# Singing Hymns with Ezra Pound in Indiana and Robert Winter in China

## H. R. Stoneback

This essay has as its provenance the keynote address at the Second International Imagism/Sixth International Richard Aldington Society Conference held at Brunnenburg Castle in June 2010.[1] In its original avatar, this essay had to perform the work of contextualization for the several days of conference papers and Imagist/Hymnagist poetry readings that followed. Although the usual process of editing conference presentations for academic publication removes traces of oral presentation, such a stripping away of a sense of occasion and wit must not be permitted to obscure the lineaments of the local and particular from which an essay is derived.

The purpose of the conference in question was to continue the conversation about Imagism that had informed the First International Imagism Conference at Brunnenburg in 2007 as well as five International Richard Aldington Society Conferences held biennially in Les Saintes-Maries-de-la-Mer France since the year 2000. As an organizer of all these events, I consistently held Imagism at the forefront of my concerns. I had also hoped to arrange a reunion of the descendants of the original Imagists. This, alas, was not to be. Catherine Aldington's illness prevented such a reunion at Brunnenburg for both the 2007 and the 2010 conferences. It was my sad duty to report at the latter conference that Catha, from her deathbed, sent greetings to all and expressed her satisfaction that "the work goes on" (5 May 2010). Catha passed away a few weeks after the conference.

In one of my last e-mail exchanges with Catha about her father and Ezra Pound, she noted, "I don't remember much although Ezra's name was often pronounced in my childhood . . . so often that writing 'Ezra' doesn't shock me. I knew also that Richard had been worried [about] the outcome of the broadcasts. Richard seemed to think Ezra didn't realize what he was doing, even less the eventual price to pay. So like other friends of Pound he agreed with Saint Elizabeths as the only way to save his life" (29 April 2007). Catha also remembered being with her father when a letter arrived from Pound announcing he was safely back in Italy. She recalled being puzzled by EP's lingo: "My father showed me the letter. I couldn't read it. Richard explained that it was not difficult for him" because they had corresponded all those years (29 April 2007). Over the course of two decades, my conversations with Catha often skirted the subject of Imagism, and more than once she proclaimed, "But isn't all good poetry in some sense Imagist?" In spite of her frequent disavowal of the importance of Imagism for her father, her own poems, which I had the privilege of publishing in several anthologies and journal issues, bore the distinct imprint of Imagism. Given my subject here—Imagism/Hymnagism—I should add that nearly a decade ago when I coined the term *Hymnagism* she roared with delight and shared memories of singing hymns with her father in—of all places—Hollywood. And we sang hymns together in the Camargue for many years.

This essay, then, is concerned with Imagism and this equally mysterious thing known as Hymnagism, and what the singing of hymns in Indiana and China might have to do with Pound and poetry everywhere. The conferees at Brunnenburg Castle in 2010 received a copy of a just-released volume of poetry entitled *Des Hymnagistes: An Anthology* (Stoneback and Nickel). This volume, which included poems by Catherine Aldington, Mary and Patrizia de Rachewiltz, Valerie Hemingway, and many other poets who were present at the conference, bears at the least a remarkable *physical* resemblance to the 1914 first edition of *Des Imagistes*, surely one of the most important twentieth-century anthologies of poetry. The facsimile appearance is, of course, an act of homage to Imagism. The *Hymnagiste* volume had its American debut at a media-blazoned literary festival in Kentucky in April 2010, and since most of the poets who read at the Brunnenburg poetry readings were represented in the volume, the conference marked the *world* première of the *Des Hymnagistes* anthology. In some sense, the conversations that ensued following the *Hymnagiste* readings marked the beginning of a replay of *Imagiste* literary history, complete with the necessary qualifications and disavowals of *Hymnagiste* identity. Just as every literary movement must have its H.D. and EP and a reluctant Aldington or Williams, I reckon every movement must also have its Amy Lowell and Skipwith Cannell and Allen Upward.

Personally, like Pound, I distrust and am wary of literary movements, even those that I spawn, especially when they begin to take on the lineaments of lit-crit and lit-historical definition and classification. I would prefer to laugh with EP and talk about being momentarily "dans le mouvemong." Or—just sing. But I note that the *Hymnagiste* act of homage to the *Imagistes* includes the facsimilitude of a "Documents" appendix that begins with an echo of Pound's words to the effect that "Twentieth-century poetry . . . [should be] austere, direct, free from emotional slither," while always simultaneously aware that, as EP insisted, "Only Emotion Endures." The documents section continues with this quote from Humphrey Carpenter: "According to Ezra . . . Amygisme had produced a 'general floppiness' among contemporary poets and . . . some 'counter-current' must be set in motion, some new element of discipline introduced. Ezra prescribed as tonic . . . the *Bay Psalm Book* (a collection of metrical psalms used by the Massachusetts Bay Colony in the mid-seventeenth century), and the use of 'rhyme and regular strophes'"(Stoneback and Nickel 93). Psalms and hymns indeed. Also in the *Des Hymnagistes* documents section, we find this from Hugh Kenner:

> All the confusion about Imagism stems from the fact that its specifications for technical hygiene are one thing, and Pound's Doctrine of the Image is another. The former, which can be followed by any talented person, help you to write what may be a trivial poem. The latter is not applicable to triviality. And an Image (this is Pound again) may be some 'Luminous Detail' out of History. . . . This principle, when he had digested it, opened the way to the *Cantos*. (*Pound Era* 186)

Cantos, yes—from *cantus*: song. Here we might add that some of the confusion about Hymnagism stems from the fact that *Hymnagiste* poets have published no manifestos, set down no narrow specifications for "technical hygiene." Hymnagism asks only that songs be made new through some knowledge of old forms and voices, through some "new element of discipline" rooted in some fashion in the much neglected form and singing voice of old hymns.

Now, to circle closer to my core hymnodic image, I note that this essay has its likely origin in the memory I recorded in a poem some years ago of my great-aunts singing hymns at the same Philadelphia Main Line Presbyterian Church and at the same time when young Ezra Pound bellowed hymns as a boy in that church in Wyncote, Pennsylvania. And this essay continued to germinate as a deep visualization of what I'd heard about Pound roaring hymns slightly off-key in the required chapel services at Wabash College in Crawfordsville, Indiana. I am well aware that I write as a poet and Hemingway scholar addressing an audience that includes Pound scholars whose extensive knowledge of Poundiana far surpasses my own. And thus I am reminded of the story of the writer and lecturer who perished in the famous Johnstown Flood. When he arrived at the Pearly Gates, St. Peter invited him to give a lecture on the Great Flood to a heavenly throng the next night. Then St. Peter added: "Uh . . . there *is one thing* you may wish to bear in mind during your talk." "What's that," the Johnstown Flood victim asked. St. Peter smiled: "Noah will be in the audience." Thus I wish to offer here with all due humility some small additions and corrections to the historical record and to do so primarily through anecdote. The reader may choose to regard the anecdotes that follow as a sign that I am approaching my anecdotage.

The first anecdote: In 1959 I dated a girl from Crawfordsville, Indiana. We both went to Asbury College in Kentucky—now called Asbury University—a small church college of the Holiness Methodist ilk. She was a senior, I was a freshman, and I was rather inordinately proud in those teenage days of my success with older women (in their *twenties*) and far too full of my triumph in dating the most attractive senior on campus. She was also one of the most talented pianists on a campus rife with piano prodigies. She had just broken up with a Wabash College guy—she seemed to think he was too "worldly." Charming word that, and quite common in certain church college circles. What did that make me—*otherworldly*? She knew Wabash College well and all of its gossip. Her family knew Wabash College faculty and administrators, so she had socialized in Wabash circles and had even played piano for required chapel services at Wabash.

She—let's call her Velma—had long black hair and she taught me many things. We played four-handed piano-duets together, and I liked watching her hands moving on the keyboard and the *frisson* of the touch that came when her hand crossed over mine in her runs to the upper notes. From Velma, I not only learned exciting new jazz chords and riffs for such songs as "Moonlight in Vermont," but also how to give piano renditions of hymns more oomph and pizzazz, how to fill the empty musical spaces with dazzle. She would play a hymn the way they did at Wabash—"draggy and Presbyterian-boring," she called it—and then play the same hymn the Asbury way, with what she called the "rhythmic sexy Methodist flamboyant runs" up and down the keyboard. And it was from Velma that I first heard about Ezra Pound's days at Wabash College.

She related Crawfordsville gossip about Pound's involvement with what they called a transvestite stripper. And she told me about his being "fired," kicked out of Wabash College, for said involvement. I report this as neither fact nor truth but as an indication of Indiana oral tradition in the 1950s. A short time later I said farewell to Velma when *I* was kicked out of Asbury College—not, I hasten to add, for involvement with transvestite strippers. I was, in the view of Asbury College, that most dangerous of things, the campus athlete-poet, the singer-songwriter-troubadour who played guitar and sang always after curfew and sometimes all night long. For that and certain other minor infractions involving girls' dormitories I had accumulated more than enough "demerits" to warrant my expulsion. Thus, in the way of young poets, my identification with Ezra Pound deepened. Before Velma told me what she told me, I had, at age 13, for example, already identified with what I thought I knew about Lord Byron; then at 14 I had identified with Shelley and Keats, but I already knew that I didn't want to die young; at age 16, of course, I had identified with Thomas Wolfe, mainly because I was by then 6-foot-6 like Wolfe. Velma had given me, at age 18, a new romantic-poet-thing to feel. The newspaper stories in those days that my father—also a poet—discussed with me about Pound and World War Two, about St. Elizabeths, about EP's return to Italy and homecoming at Brunnenburg, had far less impact on me than the knowledge that EP and I were both deemed unfit for the religious atmosphere of Midwestern/

Southern church colleges. *That was real brotherhood . . . at age 18.* But I had also discovered Imagism.

Fast forward now to China, 1984, when I was hired as Senior Fulbright Professor at China's leading institution: Peking University. Having just turned 40, I did not feel very "Senior." I was given the Fulbright appointment as a Faulkner-Hemingway expert, with a secondary reputation as a folksong specialist. And those were the courses I taught. Yet, involved as I was in matters of Modernism, Pound often came up in my discussions with Beida students and faculty. Beida, by the way, is how those in the know refer to Peking University—which is not, and must not be called, *Beijing* University. Long before my year at Beida I had, for example, studied my Vanderbilt colleague William Pratt's fine Imagist anthology for my PhD studies at Vandy, so I knew more about Imagism and Pound than I had learned from Velma years before. And by 1984, I had for more than a decade been spending a week or two on Pound in my undergraduate survey classes, using EP as a setup for *The Waste Land*, using Imagism as a point of departure for the study of all modern poetry and forcing reluctant students to memorize my recording of Pound chanting: "The thought of what America would be like / If the classics had a wide circulation / Troubles my sleep" (*Personae* 182). One student, a rock-and-roll songwriter, had a band and he set Pound's chant to music. Another talented young playwright worked Pound's litany into her play that was produced Off-Broadway. And I ended every sequence of teaching Pound with my reading of the portion of Canto 81 that I had memorized for our Pound Memorial Reading in the fall of 1972—attended by *every* member of the English faculty, regardless of politics. And when I chant "What thou lovest well remains" and "Pull down thy vanity" (Pound, *Cantos* 540-41), as I have to undergraduate students every semester since the fall of 1972, there are always some student tears and epiphanies. As one wet-eyed kid said after class this past semester: "I feel I have at last entered history and begun to live in the real world of poetry."

Thus by the time I lived in China in 1984, I was more than ready to talk about Pound, especially his profound influence on Ernest Hemingway. There was the time when I went with a group of Chinese professors, writers, and translators on an excursion to Taishan. There, in the ramshackle hotel at the top of Taishan, the most sacred mountain, I engaged in a lively discussion of the Chinese influence on Pound and Modernism. After I had made my points about Pound and Hemingway, I mostly just listened as this distinguished group of Chinese scholars and poets argued back and forth about the virtues and defects of EP's "translations" and "adaptations" from the Chinese, about "The Jewel Stairs' Grievance" and "The River-Merchant's Wife" and so forth. It was familiar enough ground to me, and I confess I was not terribly interested in their debate. I was more compelled by the views of the sacred mountain outside the window. But I was interested, and I did lead the singing with guitar and voice when, later that night, all the Chinese writers who were old enough to remember a China where God had not been officially abolished, sang along on and requested many hymns.

Like most of China's literary elite until recently, they had been educated in the pre-Mao, pre-1949 missionary schools and they knew all the hymns. One Chinese poet even suggested that there was something hymnodic about Pound's sense of form. And I was even more interested when a Chinese writer said there was an ancient retired and eccentric American professor who still lived on the Beida campus as he had for a very long time: "He loves Taishan and Pound. His name is Robert Winter and he's almost a hundred years old. He was a friend of Ezra Pound's, long ago in Indiana. You should meet him." *Yes indeed I should*, I said. My Beida colleague said we could arrange a formal visit with Winter. Or I could find Winter almost any nice day at the Summer Palace. "He will be the only 100-year old man in the lake, floating on his back smoking a cigarette." Those who know China will understand why I decided right then to find Winter at the Summer Palace lake, why I had to meet him on my own there, not with an official escort, not with a Communist Party-approved "Handler."

Soon after I returned from that Taishan Pilgrimage, I was at Yiheyuan, at the Summer Palace one hot late-May day looking for Robert Winter. He wasn't too hard to find. Kunming Lake is very large, so I walked among the pavilions and halls, the temples and towers, down the Long Gallery past the Empress's famously hideous Marble Boat, keeping my eye on the lake as I strolled. I wandered through the Garden of Nurtured Harmony, under the shadow of Longevity Hill, and then, finally, near the Jade-Belt Bridge, I saw a man floating on his back puffing away at a cigarette. I sat down on the lakeshore and waited. When he kicked his way to shore, still smoking, I took up my spot where he would come ashore. Among all the Chinese tourists and day-trippers there that day, Robert Winter and I must have been the only two westerners present. The Chinese stared at the wondrous spectacle of an old man floating on his back smoking a cigarette as he came ashore. When he had fetched his towel, dried off, and sat down on the lakeshore, I walked over to him and said:

"You must be Robert Winter. They told me I would find you here."

"Yes I'm Robert Winter and I feel absolutely *unsinkable* today." Then he began to sing: "I was sinking deep in sin, far from the peaceful shore. . . . From the waters lifted me, Now safe am I." And when he reached the chorus he belted it out— "Love lifted me, Love lifted me"—and I joined in and roared the old hymn with him. The Chinese tourists stared even more. So we met and became immediate friends over a hymn in the unlikeliest of places. When he was through singing, I said, "When I was a kid we always sang it this way: '*We* were sinking deep in sin—whoooopeee!'"

"You must be from Indiana," he said. "We sang it that way there."

"No, Kentucky."

"Next-door neighbors," he said.

"Yes, but we were better sinners and singers in Kentucky."

"Perhaps so, Lad." It was the first time anybody had called me "Lad" in a long time.

I told him who I was and he stared unblinking at me in the hard bright sunlight.

"Yes, I know who you are. Who can forget a name like Stoneback. You're that young Fulbright rebel stirring up all the trouble with your talk of Hemingway's religious vision and the secret of the values. With your singing of those gospel songs and freedom songs with that lovely wife of yours. I've seen and heard you on TV and radio. I've heard talk. I suppose since you're a writer and a Hemingway aficionado you've come to talk to me about Ezra Pound."

"I'd rather sing hymns with you," I said.

"Well said, Lad. You must come to visit me soon and we must sing and talk. I have a date for tea in five minutes. I live on the Beida campus but my place is in a secluded spot, hard to find. Since you live on campus in the Shao Yuan faculty apartments, I'll have my houseboy deliver a map to your mailbox there. Is tomorrow at 4 good for you? Will you find me?"

"Yes. And yes, I'm a good map-reader."

I watched him walk away, very solid and steady for a back-floating, cigarette-smoking, 95-year-old man. When I got back to my campus apartment that evening, his map was waiting in my mailbox.

The next afternoon, following his map, I found Robert Winter's compound in an out-of-the-way sequestered garden at the back of the lovely and extensive Beida campus. That first visit was like all subsequent visits: we talked about Beida and Chinese history first, then about Pound. He loved Ezra, he always said, and Pound was the only beacon of civilization in Crawfordsville. He was still an undergraduate (class of 1909), but he became part of Pound's circle of friends. "Without Ezra I would probably still be stuck in the Wabash Wasteland!" He said that every time I visited. He also told an unvarying version of Pound's dismissal from Wabash that involved, not a transvestite stripper, but a local school teacher to whom Pound was innocently giving language lessons in his living quarters. Winter told me that he and Pound smoked together, drank some together, discussed language and literature, sang hymns together in chapel, and later, in quiet, they composed and sang parodic versions of the hymns. (I should add that hymn-parody is an exercise familiar to anyone who has attended a church college.) Winter said Pound seemed to "love hymns, perhaps for the form, and he sang them lustily if somewhat off-key" in the required chapel services.

Winter thought that Ezra would love the fact that my wife and I were the first persons in Mao's China to sing hymns and gospel songs in our uncensored concerts that were largely folk and country music. He had seen us sing at our first major Beida concert when a near-riot erupted over our singing of gospel songs. And he said that Ezra would love the fact that the next day at the large Beida bulletin board where all the revolutions and movements of modern China had started, Mao's face, with the usual cartoon balloon with words invoking one people's campaign or another, had been replaced by life-size portraits of my wife and me, singing, with a cartoon balloon reading: "I'll fly away Oh Glory . . . Hallelujah." And Winter could not stop laughing over the fact that the required early-morning student exercise drills, conducted outdoors to some dreary loudspeaker-blaring version of "The East is Red" or some other Communist Party Hymn, had been replaced with student calisthenics to the gospel hymns of *Stoney & Sparrow* (our stage name) broadcast with great amplitude over the entire campus. Winter said that atheists sometimes were the most emotional singers of hymns. He was, he insisted, a lifelong atheist, but he loved the hymns now, the hymns that were one thing when you were a boy trapped in the pietistic wastelands of mid-America and quite another thing when you were an old man in a far country. Most visits we sang a few bars of a hymn or two. He always remembered the words.

At some point in every visit, we discussed literary history in a general way. In the notes I made in my 1984 China journal regarding my visits with Winter, there is not much about Imagism. Winter knew Pound at Wabash College, long before Imagism was announced, proclaimed, defined as a literary movement. But Winter was conversant with the tenets of Imagism, and we did discuss Pound's ideas about luminous details, about disdain for metaphor and symbol, about how the natural fact precisely observed and arranged was the sufficient vehicle to convey the emotion. My notes tell me that Winter discussed Pound and Gaudier-Brzeska, although what was said is lost in my shorthand cryptography. Occasionally, I recorded exactly things that Winter said, such as this: "An ancient man smoking a cigarette floating on his back in a lake is not a symbol of anything. It is an image, an arrangement of line and angle, plane and surface that is adequate to contain the emotion that endures only and always in the exact image." At the time, I was teaching "Big Two-Hearted River" in my Beida Hemingway Seminar. Winter seemed to know the story by heart and to regard it as Hemingway's distillation of everything he had learned from Pound. We agreed about that as we agreed on such small precise matters as the fact that Hemingway's reference to Wabash College in "Mr. and Mrs. Elliot" (*In Our Time*) was not as much a buried Pound allusion as a playful but forced salute to Pound in a story whose humor was somewhat strained.

Near the end of every visit, Winter would tease me with the familiar trick that lonely old literati use to ensure that young scholars will come back again—he would offer to show me what he called his most treasured possessions, his letters from EP. He would summon his maid-cook-housekeeper and tell her in Chinese to fetch the box with the EP letters. After a while, she would return and say the box had been misplaced. "We'll find them for your next visit," Winter always said. But I never saw the letters, if they existed. No one I knew in China had seen the letters. Then I left China. Not long after, I heard that Robert Winter had died. I have been unable to determine what disposition was made of his possessions after his death.

That is *my* story of Robert Winter and Ezra Pound, of singing hymns in Crawfordsville, Indiana and China. Robert Winter merits *one sentence* in Humphrey Carpenter's one-thousand-page biography, which reprints Winter's tribute to EP: "Without Pound I probably would now be an idiot crawling about in Crawfordsville" (74). Carpenter reprints that sentence from a letter written by Winter to a Chinese student, included in a 1984 article on Pound in Crawfordsville by James J. Wilhelm. It is mildly distressing to read in Wilhelm's article that Winter taught at *Beijing* University—since it has always been and always will be *Peking* University; it is disappointing to read Wilhelm's implication that Winter was a teaching colleague of Pound's at Wabash when in fact he was an undergraduate; and it is disconcerting to read in Wilhelm that the Robert Winter with whom I had such good conversations in *1984* died in *1983* (*Paideuma* 24-25 and *American Roots* 178-79). I like to think Robert Winter is still out at the Summer Palace, floating on his back in Kunming Lake, puffing away on a cigarette. And that his treasured letters from Ezra will someday be found.

In sum, then, I sang hymns in China with Robert Winter, and through him, with him, I sang hymns at Wabash College in Indiana with Ezra Pound, and with my great-aunts in that Presbyterian church in Wyncote where in his boyhood Pound must have found the hymns a salutary antidote to tedious homilies, must have studied, as I did as a boy, the hymnal—that great repository of form complete with a metrical index. And I can hear Pound singing: the thought of what America would be like if the *hymns* still had a wide circulation—ah well, it troubles my sleep.

## Notes

1. This conference had the affiliated support of the Elizabeth Madox Roberts Society and the Nick Adams Society. Roberts, unfamiliar to many twenty-first-century readers, was an extraordinary American novelist and poet from Kentucky who was active in the 1920s and '30s. She was deeply influenced by the work of Ezra Pound. Until recently, I thought I was the first writer to christen Roberts an Imagist. But then I learned that Ford Madox Ford had long ago praised Roberts as the finest of American novelists and proclaimed her status as "*Imagiste.*" The other supporting society for this conference, the Nick Adams Society, is named after one of Ernest Hemingway's most important recurrent characters. Everyone must know by now that Hemingway was indeed an Imagist, and EP's most celebrated pupil.

## Works Cited

Aldington, Catherine. Message to the author. 29 April 2007. E-mail.

---. Message to the author. 5 May 2010. E-mail.

Carpenter, Humphrey. *A Serious Character: The Life of Ezra Pound.* New York: Delta, 1988. Print.

Kenner, Hugh. *The Pound Era.* Berkeley: U of California P, 1971. Print.

Pound, Ezra. *The Cantos of Ezra Pound.* New York: New Directions, 1995. Print.

---. *Personae: The Shorter Poems of Ezra Pound.* Rev. ed. Ed. Lea Baechler and A. Walton Litz. New York: New Directions, 1990. Print.

Stoneback, H. R. ed. *A Garland of Poems for Catherine Aldington.* West Park, NY: Des Hymnagistes P, 2006. Print.

---., and Matthew Nickel, eds. *Des Hymnagistes: An Anthology.* Lafayette, LA: Des Hymnagistes P, 2010. Print.

---., and Matthew Nickel, eds. *What Thou Lovest Well Remains: Poems c/o Brunnenburg Castle.* West Park, NY: Des Hymnagistes P, 2007. Print.

Wilhelm, James J. "On the Trail of the 'One' Crawfordsville Incident or, The Poet in Hoosierland." *Paideuma* 13:1 (1984): 11-47. Print.

---. *The American Roots of Ezra Pound.* New York: Garland, 1985. Print.

# Notes on Contributors

ANDERSON D. ARAUJO is Assistant Professor of English at the University of British Columbia, Okanagan campus. He has published articles on Ezra Pound, T. S. Eliot, Virginia Woolf, and avant-garde movements. He is currently producing an annotated edition of Pound's *Guide to Kulchur* and a monograph on modernist cultural politics.

HELEN CARR is an Emeritus Professor in the Department of English and Comparative Literature, Goldsmiths, University of London. She is the author of *The Verse Revolutionaries: Ezra Pound, H.D. and the Imagists* (Jonathan Cape, 2009) and a co-editor of the journal *Women: A Cultural Review*. The second edition of her book, *Jean Rhys*, was published earlier this year.

JOHN GERY, Research Professor at the University of New Orleans, directs the Ezra Pound Center for Literature, Brunnenburg, Italy. His seven books of poetry include *The Enemies of Leisure* (1995), *Davenport's Version* (2003), *A Gallery of Ghosts* (2008), and *Have at You Now!* (forthcoming 2014). He has recently co-edited two anthologies of poetry, *The Poets of the Sala Capizucchi* (with Caterina Ricciardi and Massimo Bacigalupo, 2011), and *In Place of Love and Country* (with Richard Parker, 2013), as well as *Ezra Pound, Ends and Beginnings: Essays and Poems* (with William Pratt, 2011).

CHRISTOS HADJIYIANNIS is a Research Fellow in English Literature at Wolfson College, University of Oxford, where he is working on a project on modernism and Conservatism, focusing specifically on the writings of T. E. Hulme, Edward Storer, J. M. Kennedy, and A. M. Ludovici.

DANIEL KEMPTON is Associate Professor of English at SUNY New Paltz. He is a founding member of the International Richard Aldington Society and co-editor (with H. R. Stoneback) of four volumes of proceedings from that society's biennial conference. He has published articles on the medievalism of Aldington and Ezra Pound.

JUSTIN KISHBAUGH is a doctoral candidate at Duquesne University, where he is completing a dissertation on Ezra Pound, Imagism, and the Imagist Anthologies. He has presented papers at both the International Richard Aldington/Imagism conference and the Ezra Pound International Conference. He recently published a chapbook of poetry entitled "For the Blue Flash" and has another article on Imagism and Richard Aldington due to appear in a forthcoming issue of *Florida English*.

IAN S. MacNIVEN, an Emeritus Professor of English who retired from the SUNY Maritime College in 2000, wrote the authorized biography of Lawrence Durrell and edited two collections of Durrell's correspondence (with Richard Aldington and Henry Miller). His authorized biography of James Laughlin, poet and founder of the New Directions Publishing Corporation, will be published by Farrar, Straus and Giroux in 2014.

BRAD McDUFFIE is a Lecturer in English at Nyack College. His book, *Teaching Salinger's Nine Stories*, was published in the fall of 2011, his article "For Ernest, With Love and Squalor: The Influence of Ernest Hemingway on the Life and Work of J. D. Salinger" appeared in the spring 2011 edition of *The Hemingway Review*, and his first book of poems, *And the West Was Not So Far Away*, was published in 2009. He is currently finishing his PhD in English at Indiana University of Pennsylvania.

SHELLEY PUHAK is Assistant Professor at Notre Dame of Maryland University. She is the author of two collections of poetry: *Guinevere in Baltimore*, selected by Charles Simic for the 2013 Anthony Hecht Prize, and *Stalin in Aruba*, awarded the 2010 Towson Prize for Literature.

MAX SAUNDERS is Director of the Arts and Humanities Research Institute, Professor of English and Co-Director of the Centre for Life-Writing Research at King's College London, where he teaches modern literature. He studied at the universities of Cambridge and Harvard, and was a Fellow of Selwyn College, Cambridge. He is the author of *Ford Madox Ford: A Dual Life*, 2 vols. (Oxford University Press, 1996) and *Self Impression: Life-Writing, Autobiografiction, and the Forms of Modern Literature* (Oxford University Press, 2010); and the editor of five volumes of Ford's writing, including an annotated critical edition of *Some Do Not . . .* (Carcanet, 2010), the first volume of *Parade's End*.

ALEX SHAKEPEARE is an Adjunct Instructor at Boston College, where he defended his dissertation, "Robert Lowell, Lyric and Life," in the spring of 2013. He is the author of essays on Ernest Hemingway, Nathaniel Hawthorne, and Geoffrey Hill, among others.

H. R. STONEBACK is Distinguished Professor of English at SUNY New Paltz. Poet and literary critic, he has published hundreds of essays on American, British, Chinese, and French literature and is the author or editor of 30 books, roughly half literary criticism, half poetry. Recent volumes include *Reading Hemingway's The Sun Also Rises* (Kent State University Press, 2007) and *Voices of Women Singing* (Codhill Press, 2011).

ROY VERSPOOR is an Adjunct Instructor at Suffolk County Community College. He has presented papers at the conferences of the South Atlantic Modern Language Association and the Elizabeth Madox Roberts Society in addition to the two International Richard Aldington/Imagism conferences. Another article on Imagism is forthcoming in *Florida English*.

J. T. WELSCH is Lecturer in English Literature and Creative Writing at York St. John University in the UK. He completed a PhD at the University of Manchester in 2010 on "The Linguistic Subject of William Carlos Williams' Spring and All," and has published three chapbooks of his own poetry.

# INDEX

and Impressionism, xiv, 40-41, 95-103,
126
influence of, xv, 67, 135-45, 149-55, 157-
61, 164-65, 171, 172-73, 176-77, 177n1
and language, 1-3, 18-19, 48
and light, 43n6, 68-71, 72, 73-74, 81
*logopoeia/phanopoiea* in works of, 68, 81,
82, 110-12, 116, 118
and "luminous detail," 53-54, 72, 176
and *melopoeia*, 81-82, 109-10
and microscopics, 66-71
and music, 78, 81, 83-89, 163, 177
and politics, 3-5, 7-9, 25
and the radiant node, xiv, 68, 71-74
at St. Elizabeths, 159, 171
and science, xiv, 64-66, 73
and sculpture, 82, 88, 89n3
and symbolism, 37-38, 57n8, 83
and Vorticism, xiv, 47-57, 68-71, 114,
143-44
and Wabash College, xv-xvi, 170-71, 175,
176-77
Works:
   *ABC of Reading*, 68, 161
   "After Ch'u Yuan," 67
   *A Lume Spento*, 85
   "Ancient Music," 55
   "Ancient Wisdom, Rather Cosmic," 55
   *Antheil and the Treatise on Harmony*,
   79
   "Arnold Dolmetsch," 97
   "Before Sleep," 55, 68, 70
   *The Cantos*, 4, 10, 54, 55, 72, 84, 88,
   89n4, 109, 110, 159, 163, 169-70
   Individual Cantos:
   *Canto 3*, 109
   *Canto 4*, 109
   *Canto 7*, 103
   *Canto 49*, 109
   *Canto 81*, 172
   *Canto 91*, 73, 159
   *Canto 93*, 73
   *Canto 106*, 73
   *Canto 110*, 109-110, 118
   *Canto 116*, xii, 73

*Cathay*, 9, 89n4
"Cavalcanti," 73, 119n4
*Collected Shorter Poems*, 100
"The Complete Poetical Works of T. E.
   Hulme," *see* Hulme: Works
"Dogmatic Statement on the Game
   and Play of Chess," 51
"Doria," 67
"*Dubliners* and Mr. James Joyce," 102,
   104n10
*Early Writings*, 25n4, 81, 85
"Epitaphs," 55
"Et Faim Sallir Le Loup Des Boys," 54,
   55, 56
*Ezra Pound and Dorothy Shakespear*,
   42n3, 102
*Ezra Pound to His Parents: Letters
   1895-1929*, 6
"Fan-Piece for Her Imperial Lord," 8-9,
   67
"A Few Don'ts by an Imagiste," xv, 1-2,
   20, 36, 43n6, 49, 94, 115-16, 149,
   150, 152
"Fratres Minores," 51
"The Game of Chess," 68, 69-70, 72
*Gaudier-Brzeska*, 20, 50, 97, 99, 143,
   152
"Gnomic Verses," 55
*Guide to Kulchur*, 57, 112
"His Vision of a Certain Lady Post
   Mortem," 55
*Homage to Sextus Propertius*, 89n4
"How to Read," 110-11
*Hugh Selwyn Mauberley*, 95, 97, 99,
   104n5
"I Gather the Limbs of Osiris," 53-54,
   64, 65, 72, 136
"In a Station of the Metro," 4, 6, 9,
   11n4, 52, 67, 81, 82-83, 98, 112, 136-
   37, 138-39, 142, 144, 152
"In Morte De," 85
"In the Vortex," 81, 82
*Instigations*, 81
*Jefferson and/or Mussolini*, 112
"The Jewel Stairs' Grievance," 173